The Path to Peace Within

A Guide to Insight Meditation

HELEN JANDAMIT

Gateway Books, Bath, U.K.

Published 1997 by
GATEWAY BOOKS,
The Hollies, Wellow,
Bath, BA2 8QJ, U.K.

Copyright (c) 1998 by Helen Jandamit

Distributed in the U.S.A. by
Access Publishers Network
6893 Sullivan Rd, Grawn, M1 49637

Cover design by Synergie, Bristol

Text set in Goudy 10.7 on 13pt
by Oak Press, Castleton
Printed and bound by
Redwood Books of Trowbridge

British Library Cataloguing-in Publication Data:
A catalogue record for this book is
available from the British Library

ISBN 1-85860-031-6

To Ven. Phra Khru Bhavananusit
Meditation Master

Contents

Preface

Many Westerners, and people from the East too, are very interested in mind development as a means of finding peace and a
deeper understanding of life. They may, however, be wary of
organised religion.

This book is a guide to the heart-teaching of a very ancient
system of spiritual development. But it is not only intended for
Buddhists or even Buddhist sympathisers. On the other hand, it
was written for those who would like to try Vipassana or Insight
meditation practice in order to find peace within. It contains
detailed instructions for standing, walking, sitting and lying down
meditation, an indication of what benefits can be expected and
a list of possible pitfalls and how to avoid them.

These exercises can be done individually in your own home,
in a quiet place anywhere or as part of an organised retreat. In
this connection, information useful for those who are planning
to enter a meditation centre for a longer stay is also included.

Originally written as essays to complement the instruction
given at the International Buddhist Youth Seminar held at
Dhamma Sathan Vongvanij, Thailand, in 1989, this book is for
English-speaking people all over the world. As many readers
may have English as a second language, the vocabulary and syn-
tax have been kept as clear and simple as possible.

The method or practice dealt with in this book is that which was taught by the late Venerable Dhamma Theerarach Mahamuni, who was the Chief Master for Vipassana meditation in Thailand. Vipassana meditation developed within the Theravada tradition which is followed in Sri Lanka, Burma, Thailand, Cambodia, Laos and Chittagong in Bangladesh.

I would like to express my thanks to Khun Mere Siri Krinchai, Ven. Phra Khru Bhavananusit of Wat Boonsrimuneegorn and the first team of Dhammadhuta monks from the Buddhapadipa Temple in London, all of whom have been good friends and valued teachers.

H. Jandamit (Rev. Saddharma)
Bangkok, February 1997.

Opening the Doors of Perception

"If the doors of perception were cleansed, everything would appear to man as it is, infinite."   William Blake

Vipassana meditation allows the meditator to cleanse his mind of the deepest tendencies which have been subconsciously controlling his perception of the world since birth.

"I suddenly felt very happy. I felt about me a steadily rising tide of enormous joy. The warmth of the tide was glorious, as of a huge, affectionate flame. I remained intellectually conscious; that is, I was critical of my own condition, considering it, comparing it, wondering what it might mean. Never before had I attained this discriminate consciousness which functions on a plane where all discrimination seemed absurd. Then the tide ebbed slowly and I was left exhilarated, rested, refreshed."[1]

Christmas Humphreys

Here Christmas Humphreys, one of the founders of the London Buddhist Society, seeks to describe an experience both startling and wonderful. Experiences such as this are not reserved for an exclusive, mystical elite. With the application of a little mindfulness everyone can have an enhanced experience of the present moment.

Years ago when I was a student at college, I was having a coming-of-age (21st) birthday party with friends and flatmates.

Some of the students who rented the flat above had come down to join the party. I was standing looking out of a large, old-fashioned window, looking across the darkened evening city-scape, when one of them told me that we should keep the sound down, because the old man who lived in the flat below was dying. Suddenly the incongruous reality of the old man dying at the same time as I was entering upon adulthood fused together into an eruption of completeness that doubled me over with its intensity.

When, eventually, I could straighten up, the view was changed. It had broadened to encompass half the globe. Each tiny movement upon it was engaged in a cosmic dance of rightness and interaction. The crane that creaked in the far distance sang as melodiously as a lark. The child that cried in the night had a perfect right to 'be', here and now.

Of course, the intensity of the experience faded, leaving behind a world dull and segmented. Then began the search. How could this wholeness be recaptured? In my heart I knew it existed in each and every present moment, but I couldn't reach it.

Robert Linssen says, "Reality is where we are from moment to moment".[2] But how can we open ourselves to that reality? Over twenty years ago in England, instruction in meditation was almost impossible to find. I had no money to travel to the East, so the world 'here and now' became my teacher.

Perhaps, I thought, if I looked closely enough, I could find that all-encompassing oneness in the cracks in the pavement; in the acrid stench of the decomposing autumn leaves. Maybe it was there in the jarring clang of a doorbell or in the vast blue of the winter sky. Perhaps instead of moving automatically in response to a mental wish or command, if I watched each movement clearly, and each part of the movement as it was happening, perhaps then the present moment would reveal its secrets again.

Twenty years later, an important Thai meditation teacher,

Khun Mere Siri Krinchai, said the most important aim for meditators was to maintain bare awareness of the postures of the body, its movements and all sensations and thoughts that occur in the present moment.

I knew only that meditation meant looking within. Looking where within? What was going to remain constant? What could be the anchor point, the focus of awareness? The heart beat? No, that was too fast. Breathing? Yes, that would do. So I stumbled upon a method of meditation which used the patterns of breathing as a point of focus and simultaneously expanded awareness of the body.

Many years later, I was to find that this was the very method called 'Vipassana' or 'Insight' meditation. So began an adventure, a journey into awareness, both frightening and exhilarating and ultimately releasing. What I was to experience transcended all that had occurred before. Those first feelings of completeness were only a pale shadow of what was to come.

Later, in Buddhist temples, and in the university of the world, I studied Vipassana for many years. This book is a guide for those who do not have easy access to such teaching. It is meant for those who have been casting about in the dark, searching for that which will deepen and illuminate their experience of reality.

For those who see life as being full of unsatisfactoriness and suffering, and who sense that there must be a truth that transcends and gives meaning to existence; for those who wish to go into that truth, this book is a guide.

Although it is certainly possible to practise on your own, the personal guidance of a 'Good Friend in the Dhamma' is a great reassurance. The Good Friend may be a Buddhist monk or nun, or an experienced lay meditator.

The benefits of Vipassana meditation are manifold. Successful practice can lift depression, cure many stress-related diseases and, at the very least, add a little joy to life. It can help a harassed housewife cope with a family of young children. It can help a person control his temper or do well in examinations. It can help to expand and intensify an artist's perception of the world. All of those benefits are side effects of the wisdom that arises during the practice of Vipassana meditation.

The practice of Vipassana meditation enables us to become calmer and look within in order to develop wisdom and freedom.

The Way to Awakening

At the point of waking up in the morning, have you had the experience of being caught for a second between a dream state and a waking state? For a split second you are in a position to compare the two states. The dream state, that just a moment ago seemed so real and immediate, is revealed as a jumble of thoughts, unrelated or barely related to the material world and the actual situation in which we spend our waking hours. Can you imagine, by analogy, a second waking up, in which the seemingly solid and verifiable mundane world of traffic jams and bird song, of concrete high rises and mountain streams, of humdrum office routine and exultant church music, all seem to be just a tissue of mind forms only barely related to the deepest truth?

It is not that the situation has changed. The person who was dreaming is the same person who woke up. The bed and the room he was in remain the same, but the mind has opened to a new dimension of understanding. This awakening to truth, or what in Buddhism is termed 'Dhamma' is not simply a heightened or more intense sensory experience. The everyday sensory experiences I mentioned are within the realms of ordinary, mundane existence, because they are all dependent upon the contact between the sense organs and external objects. Our feelings soar to rarefied heights with the pure, clear voices of the choir as they echo and dance through the arches of the cathedral, but when the singing stops we are left with a mere memory. It is a transitory, impermanent excitation dependent upon

certain conditions and ceasing in accordance with them. However, we seek the pleasant and try to avoid the unpleasant. We
would like to keep the bird song, the mountain streams and the
oratorios, but ignore the high-rises and the traffic jams.

We feel that to surround ourselves with pleasant sensations,
that is to say, to intensify the highs and avoid the lows, would
lead to happiness. It certainly can, temporarily.

Real awakening is beyond absorption into the highs or avoidance of the lows. It is a transcendence of both, based on understanding borne of actual, experiential knowing. Highly concentrated states, accompanied by feelings of bliss or deep peace,
may arise when practising meditation. These can be extremely
uplifting experiences and may seem, compared to ordinary perception of the world, to be a kind of awakening. They are like a
helping hand along a treacherous path. They encourage and
support. They lend us strength to go on, but they are not the
ultimate aim of Buddhist practice.

The way to awakening does not consist of formal meditation
practice only. We cannot graft a little meditation on to our existing life-style and expect major changes. Meditation is not like
a multivitamin tablet taken daily to supplement our diet. The
way to awakening is the Middle Way or *Majjhima Patipada*. It
means a way of living — not simply a method of meditation.
One of the most important teachings of the Buddha is the **Four
Noble Truths** or *Cattari Ariya Saccani*, the fourth of which is
the path or the way leading to the cessation of suffering
(Dukkha): the way leading to awakening to the truth. But before talking about the Fourth Noble Truth it is logical to look at
the other three.

The First Noble Truth, **Dukkha**, is often translated as suffering or unsatisfactoriness. These are useful translations although
they fail to convey the full meaning of the term *Dukkha*. *Dukkha*
represents a whole range of experiences from mild discomfort,
such as that which makes a person shift position when sitting,
to extreme anguish. But more than this, it represents the

inherent unsatisfactoriness of all compounded things, because they have within their very nature a basic instability and impermanence. Buddhism does not deny that there can be happiness and satisfaction, but it draws attention to the fact that a state of happiness, however intense it may be, is transient. We would like happiness to remain and we feel disappointed or bereft when it passes.

The Second Noble Truth, **Samudaya**, the origin of *Dukkha*, is the wishing to hold on to that which is pleasant or to be rid of that which is unpleasant. In short, it is craving or desire rooted in ignorance of the true nature of existence. When we try to hold on to that which is pleasant, we must inevitably be disappointed and so *Dukkha* arises. On the other hand, it is not possible to shield ourselves totally from the harsh realities of life. Trying to avoid them is an impossible task comparable to trying to turn back the tides.

The Third Noble Truth, **Nirodha**, states that *Dukkha* can cease. The cessation is effected by the eradication of ignorance which is the root of suffering. When wisdom arises, ignorance (*Avijja*) is eradicated, just as when a lamp is lit, darkness is dispelled.

The Fourth Noble Truth, **Magga**, is the way leading to the cessation of suffering.

Dukkha (the First Noble Truth) is the second of the Three Characteristics of Existence. When it is translated as suffering this gives rise to the superficial impression that Buddhism is a gloomy, pessimistic religion. However, as I have tried to show above, suffering is only a partial rendition of the meaning of *Dukkha*. It also implies imperfection, impermanence and insubstantiality. If we look at the First Noble Truth in isolation, this gloomy impression can arise. In fact, it should be seen as one of the Four Noble Truths which can show the way to transcend or go beyond suffering. This transcendence is not a temporary alleviation of suffering, nor a cosmetic overlay of superficial peace, but the way to stop suffering at its root.

All living beings are subject to birth, decay, disease and death. This is evident in the cyclic changes of plant life and the steady turn of the seasons. Even the stones eventually turn to dust. The process is the same, but the time span of the change is different. Sensual pleasures and happy physical and mental states come to an end. People in the twentieth century are more acutely aware of the fact of change than ever before. The city-scape changes almost overnight. Fashions and ways of earning a living constantly change. And which of us has not come into contact with realities of twentieth century living such as lay-offs and divorces?

Being fully and directly aware of the ever-changing nature of existence is part of waking up to the truth. This is not mere intellectualisation. It is direct realisation.

Ordinary suffering is *Dukkha*. Getting what we don't want, that is, association with unpleasant conditions or persons, causes discomfort or suffering to arise in us. Separation from loved ones, wishing to have pleasant experiences or, in other words, not getting what we want, is *Dukkha*.

Realisation of the inherent unsatisfactoriness of our condition constitutes starting to wake up. As understanding deepens, we realise that we are slaves to emotions. We are always striving for the pleasant and trying to avoid the unpleasant.

According to Buddhism, a living person or being is a combination of ever-changing mental and physical forces or energies comprised of five functions or aspects: matter, feelings, perception, mental formations and consciousness; consciousness being based on the first four. These combinations of mental and physical forces are constantly changing and therefore impermanent. Whatever is impermanent is *Dukkha*. Attachment to certain aspects of a constantly changing process is futile. It leads to suffering; not simply registering the logic of this, but in experiencing it directly through practice is the beginning of awakening. In order to see how the unsatisfactoriness and suffering of *Dukkha* can be brought to an end, it is necessary to understand its nature.

We must get acquainted with it and have the courage to face it honestly.

The Second Noble Truth, *Samudaya,* is the origin of unsatisfactoriness. It is the clinging to or craving for pleasant sensations. It is the desire either for becoming or for extinction. If there is a loud, rasping noise and we want it to stop, we tense up, we try unsuccessfully to ignore the noise, this sets up negative, stressful conditions within us, we get a headache... *Dukkha* has arisen.

But if we can be aware of the sound simply as sound, without mentally labelling it as pleasant or unpleasant, without the habitual mental reactions of 'like' and 'dislike' coming into play, then the physical resistance does not arise, there is no tensing up. In this case *Dukkha* does not arise. How can we reach this state of equanimity, in which all sound is simply sound, where illusions and delusions are stripped from experience and we are left with a direct realisation of truth?

The Third Noble Truth states that *Dukkha* can cease. *Nirodha* means the Cessation of *Dukkha.* If craving causes *Dukkha,* then if it is overcome there will be no *Dukkha.* The Buddha says, "If craving, anger and delusion are given up, man aims neither at his own ruin nor at the ruin of others, nor at the ruin of both, and he experiences no mental pain or grief. This is **Nibbana**, immediate, visible in this life, inviting, attractive and comprehensible to the wise".

Nibbana cannot be adequately described through the limited constraints of words. It cannot be completely grasped by the intellect. It is not merely to be understood; it is to be realised. The understanding we can get of Nibbana through the medium of words is as much like the true nature of Nibbana as a shadow cast on the ground is like a tree. There may be some superficial resemblance to the general form, seen from a limited viewpoint, but it does not convey the colour and texture of the tree. It gives only a distorted approximation of its size. It does not even hint at the living reality of the tree and of the complex processes going on within it.

In the Udana the Buddha describes *Nibbana* in this way:

> Where neither water nor yet earth
> Nor fire nor air gain a foothold.
> There gleam no stars, no sun sheds light.
> There shines no moon, yet there no darkness reigns.
> When a sage, a Brahmin, has come to know this
> For himself through his own experience.
> Then he is freed from form and formless,
> Freed from pleasure and from pain.

The Buddha realised *Nibbana*. He became the Awakened One, *Bhagavan*, and through the guidance of his teaching, many of his disciples were also able to realise Nibbana. The Buddha said that where there were people genuinely practising the Dhamma, the world would not be without *Arahants* (Enlightened Beings). Nibbana is attainable within this life. So how can we practise? What is the way to awakening?

Summarised into its simplest form it is:

> Do good
> Avoid evil
> Purify the mind

Westerners often think it is possible to do only the third — purify the mind — in other words 'meditate', without making any other changes to their life-style. It is possible to add a topping of superficial tranquillity to an existing life-style. But it remains superficial. Real awakening is unlikely to take place in such a situation. The way to awakening was given by the Buddha in detail. He set out a path with eight components. This is called **The Noble Eightfold Path**, which teaches us how to do good, avoid evil and purify the mind. To do good and avoid evil means to have a firm moral base to guide our actions. To do good, we need to act with compassion, sympathy, loving kindness and fairness to all beings. The Buddha gave his teaching "for the good of the many, for the happiness of the many, out of compassion for the world".

Three components of the Noble Eightfold Path: Right Speech (*Samma Vaca*), Right Action (*Samma Kammanta*) and Right Livelihood (*Samma Ajiva*) give us further guidance so that we can build up a firm moral base to facilitate our progress. This is termed ethical conduct or *Sila*. It is built on the vast conception of universal love and compassion for all living beings. For lay people it means keeping the five precepts.

Right Speech means to abstain from telling lies, from backbiting and slander. It means not using harsh, abusive or impolite language, and not indulging in foolish babble and gossip. In its positive aspect it means that one should speak the truth in a friendly, benevolent way. **Right Action** promotes moral, honourable and peaceful conduct. We should abstain from killing and stealing, from dishonesty and sexual misconduct. **Right Livelihood** means that one should avoid making one's living through a profession that brings harm to yourself or to others, such as trading in arms or intoxicating drinks. Buddhist ethical and moral conduct aims at promoting harmony and happiness for the individual and for society. This moral base is indispensable for all higher attainments.

The next three components of the Noble Eightfold Path are **Right Effort**, **Right Mindfulness** and **Right Concentration**. These constitute the factors needed to purify the mind. With a balanced application of effort, mindfulness and concentration, wisdom can arise.

Samatha-Vipassana meditation when practised by someone who is keeping the five precepts can allow a waking up to the truth. Effort, concentration and mindfulness can lead to a direct, experiential knowing of the real nature of existence. When we have a firm, moral base and we practise meditation, the truth that we awaken to is called Insight Wisdom and the remaining two components of the Noble Eightfold Path. **Right Thought** (*Samma Sankappa*) and **Right Understanding** (*Samma Ditti*), together constitute wisdom. It is wisdom, or insight into truth, which is the aim of awakening. So if we wish to awaken from our unsatisfactory, ever-changing, ceaselessly-shifting prison of sensations into the calm, pure, direct understanding of a new dimension of existence, we need to live without harming others or ourselves and to develop our minds.

We can develop our minds through the practice of meditation. It takes time and application. But through this practice, real awakening can take place — right here and now in this present life. The sleeper who woke up was the same person when he was dreaming as he was when awake. The one who awakens to truth is still the same person, but now understanding has arisen; the suffering has fallen away. It is comparable to coming out of the turmoil of a bad dream into the reassurance of the primal home. As the eye of the *Dhamma* opens, awakening *is*, here and now.

Insight and Calmness Meditation

Vipassana meditation is usually called Insight meditation. It is the method of practice discovered by the Lord Buddha which led to his enlightenment over 2,500 years ago. There are two types of meditation practised by Buddhists: Vipassana and Samatha.

Vipassana is the Pali name for Insight meditation, and *Samatha* translates as Calmness. The implication is that these two methods of meditation or mind development are inherently different, but in fact they often merge together. Vipassana meditation is dependent upon a certain level of concentration which in formal meditation practice is built up by way of Calmness meditation techniques. It is also possible to follow Samatha meditation to the stage of deep absorption first and then to move to Vipassana. The Buddha himself studied yoga and Calmness meditation for six years with renowned teachers in India, before realising that the path to Nibbana must lie outside the pursuit of absorptions. He then practised Vipassana for just one day — the full moon day of May — and gained enlightenment.

When practising Samatha or Calmness meditation the meditator concentrates on one object; while in Vipassana, all that occurs in the present moment is clearly observed as it comes into existence, has being and passes away. The attitude of the meditator is one of allowance, without prejudice or bias. In order to observe clearly however, it is necessary to hold the object of attention in mind long enough to observe its essential characteristics. To do this, one must use trained concentration because, without it, attention jumps around from object to object, never really focusing clearly on any one of them.

Samatha or Calmness meditation, a system that pre-dates Buddhism, is a very efficient way of developing concentration. There are altogether forty subjects of Samatha practice used in Buddhist meditation to control and still the movements of the mind. When following this form of meditation, very deep states of absorption, termed *jhanas* may be experienced.

The forty meditation objects may be subdivided into seven main groups. The first group to be considered here is the **Ten Kasinas** which contain, for example, meditation on various colours or on light. On the walls of temples, you can see discs of primary colours which are used to aid this kind of meditation. When I was a child, I used to practise this form of meditation spontaneously, without knowing it. I would play in the grass in the garden and watch insects crawling along the blades of grass. I would smell the warm, damp earth, feel the crunch of crushed blades of grass beneath my body, then I would look up and see a blue flower against the blue sky and become totally absorbed in the blueness. There was the radiant blueness of the sky inter-acting with the absorbent blueness of the flower petals. I would not notice anything except the blueness.

The ten Kasinas are: earth device *(Pathavi Kasina)*; water device *(Apo Kasina)*; fire device *(Tejo Kasina)*; air device *(Vayo Kasina)*; red device *(Lohita Kasina)*; blue device *(Nila Kasina)*; yellow device *(Pita Kasina)*; white device *(Odata Kasina)*; space device *(Akasa Kasina)*; light device *(Aloka Kasina)*.

The second group is the **Ten Asubhas** (objects of impurity); e.g. a swollen corpse or a skeleton. In meditation temples you can see full colour photographs of corpses, and some teachers take their students on visits to the morgue. The aim of this, to quote Phra Debvedi, is to apply "what is seen, to oneself, reflecting that one's own body must meet a similar fate".[3]

In all cases, the object of meditation should be appropriate for the meditator. This may not always be so. A lady I know was taken by her teacher to look at corpses, but this didn't have the desired result because, as she had always had a thwarted desire to be a doctor, she became fascinated by the internal organs of the bodies.

The third group of meditation objects used in Samatha meditation is the **Six Anussatis** (recollections). This group represents meditation upon a concept or an idea and comes very close to the Christian idea of contemplation. The Anussatis include such subjects as 'the Recollection of the Buddha' and 'the Recollection of Morality'. The six Anussatis are considered together with the **Four Satis**, making a group of ten altogether. The four Satis are concerned with mindfulness: mindfulness of breathing, of death, of the body and of tranquillity.

The fourth group of meditation objects is recollection upon the **Four Brahmaviharas** or 'excellent qualities'. These are loving kindness, compassion, sympathetic joy and equanimity. At the end of a Vipassana session, when you send out loving kindness (Metta) to all sentient beings, you use the excellent qualities as the object of meditation. In practice this means visualising people close to you and sending out feelings of loving kindness to them, then extending the range of attention to acquaintances, strangers, human beings in general, all sentient beings and so on, radiating loving kindness to them all.

The fifth group is composed of the **Four Formless Spheres**. These are the spheres of Infinite Space, of Infinite Consciousness, of Nothingness and of Neither Perception Nor Non-Perception. The Buddhist cosmology is conceived in terms of **thirty-one planes of existence**, and it is held that if a meditator is absorbed into one of these Formless Spheres at the moment of death, he will be reborn in one of the more refined heavenly planes.

The Perception of the Loathsomeness of Nutriment constitutes the thirty-ninth object of meditation. Those attending a meditation retreat are encouraged to recollect the purpose of food before they eat. They notice each small sub-movement involved in lifting food, putting it in the mouth, tasting it, chewing it, swallowing it and try to be aware of its movement down to the stomach.

The final Samatha meditation object is the analysis of the four elements, familiar to Westerners as earth, air, fire and water.

Here is a typical calming down exercise that is used as a fore-runner to Vipassana practice. It is called *Anapanasati* or mindfulness of breathing. Watch the breath at the nostrils. As you breathe in, you say in mind 'one', as you breathe out, you say in mind 'one' again. Then as you breathe in, you say in mind 'two' and as you breathe out, you say in mind 'two' again. Continue to ten.

In Samatha meditation, the aim is one-pointedness and absorption into the *jhanic* states, which are often extremely blissful. It is also possible to develop various mental powers such as phenomenal memory, telepathy and prescience. This can be seen as an advantage or as a trap for the unwary, depending on the ultimate aim of the meditator.

Seen in terms of Vipassana, the aim to gain supernatural powers is based on the wish to enhance one's 'self', and so it would be a hindrance to a practice which enables one to become aware of non-self (*Anatta*). However in practice, as the meditator's mind becomes calmer and clearer, he or she may spontaneously give up the desire for supernatural powers. The conditions of each of our lives are different; we have different ways to connect with the path to realisation.

The objects of Vipassana meditation are: the position of the body at the present moment, as well as all sensations, emotions and thoughts resulting from contact between body, mind and the environment, or the internal interaction between sensations and mental processes — at the point when they occur. In Samatha meditation, you would choose to develop concentration until you reached absorption (*jhana*), before possibly developing Vipassana. But in *Satipatthana Vipassana* you only develop enough concentration to be able to hold the objects of meditation firmly in mind so that their essential characteristics can be noticed. This level of concentration is called Access Concentration or in Pali *Upacara Samadhi*.

'Access concentration' is characterised by various phenomena such as seeing bright lights and beautiful images, having feelings of expansion and contraction of the body, numbness, feelings of flying, of great peace and blissful happiness. However, these should be seen as signs that the practice is deepening and concentration is improving, not as ends in themselves. You are encouraged not to be attached to them.

What does 'Insight' really mean? Buddhadasa Bhikhu describes it as, "The expression 'insight into the true nature of things' refers to seeing transience, unsatisfactoriness and non-selfhood; seeing that no thing is worth getting, no thing is worth being, seeing that no object whatsoever should be grasped at and clung to as being a self or as belonging to self; as being good or bad, attractive or repulsive".[4]

In Samatha meditation you may become absorbed into blissful states, but in Vipassana you may experience bliss without becoming attached to or absorbed into it, and so you can progress to deeper states and finer awareness. In Vipassana the aim is freedom; freedom from the burden of suffering. It is gained through Insight Wisdom. As mindfulness and concentration develop in a state of optimum balance, and if there is enough energy and clear comprehension *(Sampajanna)*, then Insight Wisdom can arise.

In Vipassana meditation, concentration and energy levels are increased by the practice of walking meditation and by continuous mindfulness of the postures and positions of the body. The Pali term for these is *Iriyapatha*. In Samatha meditation absorption is usually facilitated in a static position, typically sitting in the lotus position.

In Insight meditation the aim is neither forcibly to exclude sensations or thoughts, nor to repress them, but to see clearly how they arise, have being and pass away. A certain level of concentration and energy is necessary to keep them in our sphere of attention. Without this level of concentration our minds jump all over the place, never attending fully to any one object. This is often described as a 'monkey mind'. We need to give the 'monkey' a definitive task to do, so that his attention span increases and control improves. It is very difficult to stop your mind 'jumping around' simply by an effort of will. The method used in Insight Vipassana meditation, of slowing down movements and making simple mental acknowledgements, is a very effective tool to enable us to gain stability, unshakeability and equilibrium.

In Vipassana you will clearly perceive all that occurs in the present moment in 'this fathom-long body'. Because you are not attached to anything, it is possible to be aware of the deepest tendencies within. It is possible to be clearly aware of the very root of both attachment and aversion to whatever occurs; and through seeing clearly eradicate these tendencies at the point where they originate. In Buddhism this is termed the 'eradication of defilements'. An enlightened being is one who has eradicated all defilements. He or she is free from their controlling influence.

Through unbiased, non-prejudiced and clear awareness it is possible to see the process by which we become entangled in attachments. This 'seeing' has the meaning of being aware, or of understanding. It is mental in that there is bare awareness, but it is not limited to the narrow confines of thought. It is experiential in that feelings arise and are not ignored, but it is not absorption into sensations, however rarefied they may be. Through clear comprehension based on mindfulness and concentration, it is possible for attachments and aversions to untangle themselves. The deepest tendencies of the mind are seen for what they really are, so they lose their power to control. In Samatha meditation, because concentration is fixed on an object outside our experience of the present moment — for example, the colour yellow, or analysis of the four elements — it is not possible to eradicate defilements.

It is certainly possible through discipline to live a moral, pure life, but the defilements still remain as latent tendencies. The 'Four Foundations of Mindfulness', or *Satipatthana*, is considered to incorporate both Samatha (Calmness) meditation and Vipassana (Insight) meditation. Combining concentration built up through Samatha meditation with the wisdom developed in Vipassana meditation is the way to real freedom.

Looking Within

The orange-robed figure sits immobile at the front of the room. Sunlight from the high windows slices the warm evening air. A young man sits in silence with eyes closed and legs crossed, a foam mat cushioning him from the cool floor. He is surrounded by bird song and the muted rumble of far-away traffic sounds.

As he breathes, he struggles to concentrate on the movement of the abdomen. Mentally he repeats "**Rising; falling; rising**. I wonder if I am doing this correctly? Did I remember to lock the door? I'm not concentrating. **Rising; falling**. That bird sings beautifully, just like Barbra Streisand. What is the name of that song I like? Yesterday? No. **Rising; falling**. My knee hurts. Should I move? Should I ignore it? Pay attention!"

The mind of a person who is just beginning to meditate is like a monkey. It jumps around following external stimuli: a sound, a vibration, a change in the quality of light. It follows patterns of word association and familiar emotional tendencies.

A meditator from America commented on her experience during a retreat. "One of the things that I learned was getting in touch with 'the moment'. Rather than letting my mind wander, or think about tomorrow or daydream, I learned the importance of living in the moment."

What happens when you practise on a retreat? Usually *Dhamma* talks are given after morning and evening chanting, to give the participants some knowledge of the Buddhist texts. It is necessary to have a balance between theory and practice.

Theory is like a map that we can look at to make informed decisions about which route to take. But it is not until we make the actual journey that we can really get to know the new area. On the other hand, if we travel without a map, it is very easy to lose our way.

As the sun rises and sets, and the scent of incense drifts through the hall, the voices of the monks and nuns blend to pay respect to the Triple Gem: the Buddha, the Dhamma and the Sangha.

The Buddha, the great teacher who was able to reach enlightenment by his own efforts and also to teach the way to enlightenment to others; the *Dhamma*, which can either be interpreted as the truth within the Buddhist teachings or more narrowly as the Buddhist texts; and the *Sangha*. The Sangha really means those followers of the Buddha who were able to reach enlightenment. It can also be taken to mean all the followers of the Buddha. In Thailand it is usually understood to mean the community of monks.

Formal practice focuses on four positions: standing, walking, sitting and lying down. Walking meditation is alternated with sitting meditation, and the length of practice at each session is gradually increased. In sitting meditation the meditators focus on breathing. They watch the movements of the abdomen as they breathe naturally. By watching the breathing and synchronously making mental acknowledgments of disturbances, the mind gradually stills. It is easy to be aware of anything that comes into a clear mind. The main aim of Vipassana is not to develop states of absorption which exclude the meditator from the experiential world. Someone who is in a state of deep absorption, termed *jhana* state, will not feel it if they are burned or pricked with a pin. In Vipassana, gradually concentration increases and the mind becomes clearer.

Watching the breath gradually becomes like a white background. If a speck of dust is placed on a white background, it is easier to see its form than if it is placed on a dusty surface. As practice continues and as concentration and energy increase further, it is like putting that speck of dust under a magnifying glass — and it is far easier to see its outline and shape. As practice deepens, concentration becomes like a microscope with energy lighting the object of meditation. The structure of the speck of dust begins to reveal itself; with ever-deepening concentration and unwavering effort, the electron microscope of energy and concentration sees only wave formations of energy... Where is that speck of dust now? Organic matter reveals its true nature. In the same way, in Vipassana practice, the mind/body process is put under the microscope of awareness until its true nature is revealed and insight into truth occurs.

How does it feel when the finely-tuned mind touches peace and tranquillity within? "I value the silence and the peace that I have found in the last few days — more peace than at any other time in my life", said a meditator from New Zealand.

The orange-robed monk sits immobile at the front of the hall. In the high-ceilinged room all is silent. The young man wrestles to stay with the movements of the abdomen as he breathes naturally and freely. He attends to the breath, but he does not force concentration.

Buddhism is the Middle Way. We try hard enough but not too hard. Without the compunction to stay with the breath constantly, the mind relaxes just enough to make the task easier. He mentally acknowledges the movements as they occur, **Rising; falling; rising; falling; rising; falling; I** wonder..... **Thinking; thinking; thinking**. He gently brings his attention back to rising and falling again. "That bird sings beautifully." **Hearing; hearing; hearing.** The acknowledgment is made and he gently brings his attention back to the movements of the abdomen again. The attention span increases naturally as the space between the distractions extends; the young man begins to feel very relaxed, yet alert. He feels light and full of happiness. All that occurs is seen clearly without bias or prejudice, acknowledged and allowed to pass. In this way the innate peace and freedom within the present moment is seen and experienced.

Sometimes he feels as if he is floating in a sea of radiant light, sometimes his whole being is suffused with deepest blue. Sometimes his form seems to encompass the universe. Sometimes fears that he has never acknowledged before come into his awareness, and he deals with them in the same way as he would the song of a bird. He acknowledges them, sees them clearly and lets them go. In this way he can stay in peace.

What to Do at a Vipassana Meditation Centre

If you go to a Vipassana meditation centre you will be expected to keep the Eight Precepts, to wear white clothes and to follow the instructions of your teacher diligently. When you enter a meditation centre and you ask the meditation instructor for permission to practise meditation at the centre, the instructor will expect you to repeat the Eight Precepts and to agree to keep them during the period of seclusion.

THE EIGHT PRECEPTS

The Eight Precepts or '*Uposatha-Sila*' consist of:

1) Abstinence from killing any living beings.
2) Abstinence from stealing.
3) Abstinence from unchastity.
4) Abstinence from false speech.
5) Abstinence from intoxicants.
6) Abstinence from eating solid food after mid-day.
7) Abstinence from dancing, singing, music and shows, from garlands, perfumes, cosmetics, adornment etc.
8) Abstinence from luxurious and high seats and beds.

These eight precepts constitute a firm base to facilitate the intensive practice of Vipassana Insight meditation.

PAYING HOMAGE TO THE TRIPLE GEM

After asking for the Five or Eight Precepts, and repeating them after your teacher, the meditator pays homage to the Triple Gem in this way:

"Imaham Bhagava attabhavam Tumhakam pariccajami."

"Master, may I pay homage for the purpose of practising Insight meditation from this moment on?"

The meditator pays respect to the instructor saying:

"Imaham Ajariya attabhavam Tumhakam pariccajami."

"Venerable teacher, may I show respect to you, for the purpose of practising Insight meditation from this moment on?"

The meditator asks for instruction as follows:

"Nibbanassa me bhante sacchikaranatthaya kammatthanam dehi."

"Master, will you give me instruction for Insight meditation, so that I may comprehend the Path, the Fruition and Nibbana later?"

The meditator then extends 'Loving Kindness' *(Metta)* to all beings in a way such as this:

"May I and all beings be happy, free from suffering, free from longing for revenge, free from troubles, difficulties and dangers, and be protected from all misfortune. May no being suffer loss. All beings have their own *Kamma*, have *Kamma* as origin; have *Kamma* as heredity; have *Kamma* as refuge — for whatever *Kamma* one performs, be it good or bad, returns to one."

Then the meditator contemplates death thus: "Our lives are transient and death is certain. That being so, we are fortunate to have entered upon the practice of Insight meditation on this occasion, because now we have not been born in vain and have not missed the opportunity to practise the Dhamma."

PREPARING FOR MEDITATION

The instructor will then assign various walking, sitting and lying down exercises which gradually build up concentration and energy levels. The meditator's mindfulness, or '*Sati*', also increases. It is important to bear in mind that Vipassana meditation does not cease at the completion of, for instance, a thirty-minute period of sitting meditation. Conversely, mindfulness should be maintained at all times, not only when carrying out specific walking or sitting exercises. Therefore you should try to be aware of every movement you make, every thought that arises, each sound that occurs, and be mindful when eating, drinking, getting dressed and so on.

However, at the start of a meditation retreat this is difficult in practice. We have years of conditioning to overcome. We would not be able to function under the sensory overload experienced daily in a city without a kind of censorship to filter out our awareness of much that is occurring. This leaves just enough information to enable us to deal with a task, such as crossing a six-lane highway. Usually these filters operate for most of our lives. We are living in a room with the curtains drawn. We have a very 'partial' view of existence. When mindfulness increases, the curtains are gradually drawn back and our experience of the 'here and now' becomes immeasurably richer, and insight gradually arises into the real nature of existence.

Now let me give you some very simple instructions for the first day of practice of Vipassana meditation. You are advised to wear comfortable clothes which are neither too loose nor too tight. Thai meditators who stay at the temple and keep the 'Eight Precepts' usually wear white clothes to signify their homelessness and purity. However, it is not necessary to wear white.

All the following exercises should be regarded as methods of increasing mindfulness, concentration and energy. The aim is to become clearly aware of all that is experienced at the present moment. It is not necessary to follow the movements rigidly. What is essential is that you focus and maintain mindfulness on all that arises, all that is experienced in the present moment.

However, some confusion may arise if instructions are too general. We need a clear system of signs, or else an inexperienced meditator may become lost in the vastness of sensations and thoughts.

For this reason very detailed instructions for each of the exercises are given. If, however, your movements (e.g. in the walking exercises) vary slightly from the standard ones, but mindfulness is maintained at all times, the exercise is still appropriate and will give benefit. The aim is not a tightly synchronised slow motion ballet; it is systematically to open awareness of the present moment and all that it contains.

Detailed instructions will be given for the first walking exercise. There are six of them, in which awareness of the movement of the feet becomes progressively refined. In the first exercise the raising, moving and lowering of each foot is one movement. In the second, the movement is seen in two stages; in the third, there are three stages, and so on.

The First Walking Exercise

Before walking, stand erect with your legs straight, your feet close together and your hands at your sides. Lift your left hand, and mindfully put it in the chosen position. Move slowly, feeling the movement distinctly and make the following mental acknowledgements synchronously with the movements. As you lift your left arm, say in your mind (or out loud if you are practising with a group) '**lifting**'; as you move your forearm towards your body, say silently '**moving towards**'; and as you rest your hand on your abdomen, say in mind '**setting down**'. Do the same as you move your right arm.

THE POSITION OF THE HANDS

Several hand positions are recommended. The hands may be loosely clasped in front of you, with the arms fairly straight. Or the arms may be bent so that the hands rest on your stomach. Alternatively, your hands may be loosely clasped behind you, or the arms may be folded across your chest. If the duration of the walking exercise is fairly short, it is usually unnecessary to change the position of the hands; however, if the walking meditation is prolonged, you may change their position. Remember, though, to acknowledge in your mind '**intending to change**' three times before you start making a movement. Then as you move your arms, keep mindfulness fixed on the movement. Move one arm first followed by the other, at the same time making mental acknowledgements '**lifting; moving; setting down**'.

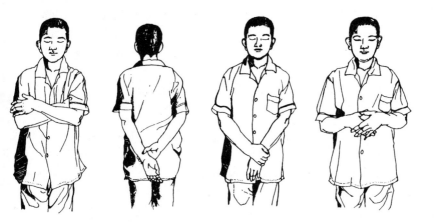

STANDING

Next, be mindful of the standing position. Try to be aware of 'body' standing, not 'I' am standing. The head should be held upright, and the eyes focused at a point about seven feet (2 metres) ahead. Make mental acknowledgements like this: focus awareness on the top of the head and make a mental sweep down the body to the soles of your feet, saying in your mind, at the same time, '**standing**'. Make a mental sweep in an upwards direction from the soles of the feet to the top of the head, saying in mind '**standing**'. A third time, make the acknowledgement '**standing**' as awareness moves down from the top of the head to the soles of the feet. At first it is quite difficult to be clearly aware of the standing posture, because there is no physical movement, but gradually the mindful mental sweep will become clearer.

WALKING

Mindfulness is now focused on the feet. Keep it there and try to be aware of the tension in your feet accompanying the desire to walk, saying in mind '**intending to walk; intending to walk; intending to walk**'. The gaze should now be lowered slightly and fixed a little in front of the foot that is moving, or up to about four feet ahead (1¼ metres). The head may be very slightly bent. It is usual to start with the right foot when practising in a group, because the instructor leads the acknowledgements out loud. Lift the right foot about three inches (8cm) from the floor; move it forward at the same level, and then set it down about five or six inches (15cm) in front of the left foot. Focus attention on the movement of the foot from the moment it is lifted until it is set down, simultaneously making the acknowledgement '**right goes thus**'. The movement of the foot is perceived as continuous, and is not divided into separate stages.

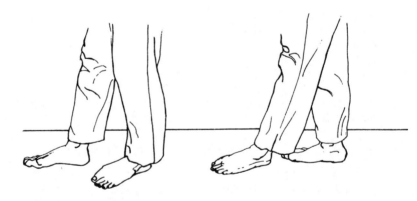

RIGHT GOES THUS   *LEFT GOES THUS*

When the left foot is being lifted, moved and set down, be aware of the movement, and simultaneously say in mind **'left goes thus'**. The acknowledgement should neither precede nor lag behind the movement. Continue walking, with awareness focused on the movement of the feet, until coming to the end of the walk space. Bring your feet together on the last step.

Be mindful of standing as before, making three acknowledgements of **'standing'**. Be clearly aware of 'body' standing, and make three mental sweeps from head to toe, toe to head, and again from head to toe.

TURNING

Keeping attention on the feet, try to feel the tension there as you become aware of the wish to turn. Make three mental acknowledgements while being aware of wanting to turn: **'intending to turn; intending to turn; intending to turn'**. For the first three walking exercises, turning is usually divided into four sections. Turn right. Move your right foot clockwise, keeping your right heel on the ground, but lifting your toes, saying in mind **'turn'** and, as you put your toes down, saying in mind **'-ing'**, the angle of movement should be about 45°.

Next lift your left foot straight up about three inches (8cm), saying in mind **'turn'**. Then place it down parallel to the right foot, saying in mind **'-ing'**. Then say **'one'**. Make four pairs of movements in this way in order to complete a 180° turn. Note that the right heel revolves on the same spot throughout.

Having turned, keeping attention focused on the movements of the feet at all times, again be mindful of **'standing'** and **'intending to walk'** as before.

The first walking exercise should be practised until you can achieve good concentration. At first the instructor may pace the exercise, calling out the acknowledgements. But when you practise privately, the acknowledgements are not made out loud, and you must pace yourself. This exercise may continue for up to thirty minutes.

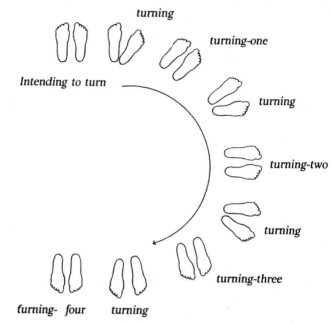

turning

turning-one

Intending to turn

turning

turning-two

turning

turning-three

turning- four   *turning*

TURNING : FOUR STAGES

While performing the walking exercises, your attention should be on the movements of the feet; not on the sound of the words. The acknowledgements should be made at the same time as the movements, not before or after them. One of the benefits of walking meditation is that it enables you to accumulate energy in order to maintain concentration more easily during the sitting exercises.

Some teachers say that the length of time spent on walking meditation should be longer than that spent on sitting meditation. Others place the emphasis differently. What is essential is that there should be a balance between the two forms. Gradually you will come to know how to maintain your own equilibrium. If you can concentrate well, but tire easily, a slightly longer time spent on walking would probably be beneficial. At first be guided by your instructor.

It is a good idea to arrange the place where you are going to sit before you start to walk, so that on completion of the walking exercise you can move slowly and mindfully into a sitting position without distractions. Imagine that you are carrying a bowl brim full of the 'Sati' or mindfulness that has been accumulated during the walking exercise. If you make unmindful movements or if your mind starts wandering during the change from walking to sitting, some of that energy will spill over the edge of the bowl and be lost.

CHANGING POSITION

As you sit down you can, if you wish, divide your movements into stages and make acknowledgements for each stage, but this is not essential as long as mindfulness is constantly maintained. If you find your mindfulness falters, the following may be helpful:

At the completion of walking meditation, stand erect and be mindful of 'body' standing as before. Attempt to be aware of 'body' by scanning from the top of your head to the soles of your feet, simultaneously saying in mind **'standing'**. Then reverse the mental sweep saying in mind **'standing'** again. As you make the acknowledgement **'standing'** for the third time, move your awareness from head to toe once more.

Next try to be aware of wanting to sit. Make three mental acknowledgements: **'intending to sit; intending to sit; intending to sit'**. After this move slowly and mindfully to your place. You may say in your mind **'right'** as your right foot moves and **'left'** as your left foot moves.

When standing in the correct position to start sitting down, move your hands mindfully to a suitable position to help you sit down. The following acknowledgements may be made: as you lift whichever hand is uppermost, say in mind '**lifting**'; as you move your arm downwards, say in mind '**dropping**'; when you let go of the tension in your arm, say in mind '**releasing**'. Do the same with the other arm.

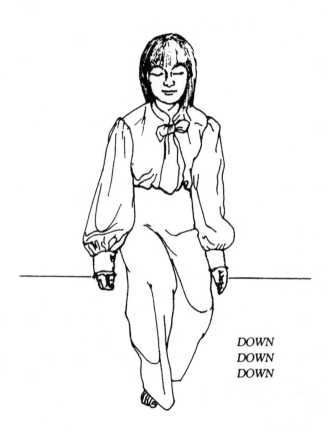

DOWN
DOWN
DOWN

If you are going to sit on the floor, you can use the sequence of movements and acknowledgements which follow later. However, if you prefer to sit on a chair, you will adjust the directions accordingly. Remember, it is not necessary to follow this series of movements in the precise order given here. The important thing is to maintain mindfulness of all your actions by making mental acknowledgements at each stage.

If you have rheumatism you may need first to put your hands down for support, as you move down. This is fine, but be clearly aware of putting your hands down as you do this, making your own private acknowledgement, even though the group in general is making a different movement.

PUTTING DOWN
TOUCHING

Here is a list of possible actions and acknowledgements to be made:

You are standing with your feet together, ready to sit down, and the mat behind you. Move your left foot backwards about 12 inches (30 cm), saying in your mind '**moving back**'. Start bending your knees, saying in mind '**down**'.

This acknowledgement can be made about five times as you move down until, as your left knee touches the ground, you make the mental acknowledgement '**touching**'. The left hand is now placed on the floor near the left knee to support the body as the

MOVING
TOUCHING

right leg is moved. As you move your hand, say in mind '**putting down; touching**'.

The right leg is now moved back so that it is in line with the left. Make the acknowledgement '**moving**' as this is happening. When the right knee touches the floor, say in mind '**touching**'. Next move the left hand backwards about nine inches (23 cm), say in mind '**moving back**' and, as the hand touches the floor, '**touching**'. As the weight moves on to the hand, say in mind '**pressing**'. Move down so that your buttocks touch your ankles, saying in mind '**sitting down**'.

As you reach out with the right hand to grasp the right ankle, say in your mind '**grasping**'.

As you lift the right foot to place it on the floor near the left knee, make the mental acknowledgement '**lifting**'. As you move

SITTING DOWN

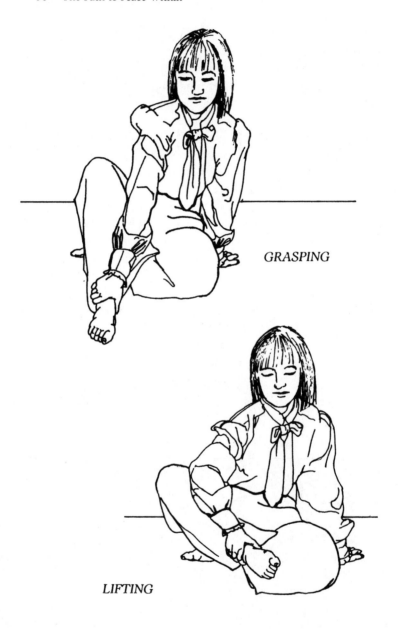

GRASPING

LIFTING

your foot across, say in mind '**moving**'. At the point where your foot touches the floor, make the acknowledgement '**setting down**'. If you wish to sit in the half or full lotus position, make the following acknowledgements as you move your legs: '**grasping; lifting; setting down**'.

When performing the sitting exercises it is essential that the spine should be erect, and the circulation unobstructed. It is not necessary to sit in a full lotus position or even cross-legged, although these positions are very stable and easy to maintain. Older people or Westerners unused to sitting on the floor may prefer a chair. However, your back should be straight and not supported by the chair back, and there should be ample room to rest the arms with the hands in the correct position. They should be held loosely on the lap with the left hand on the right hand. The tips of the thumbs may be touching. So when moving your

hands to the right position again try to maintain mindfulness like this:

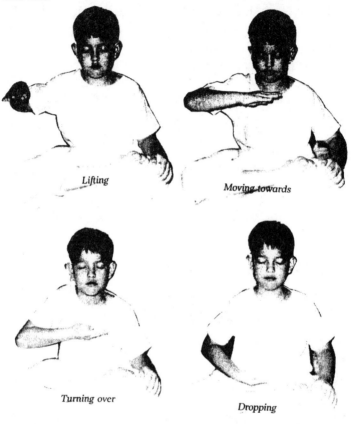

Lifting

Moving towards

Turning over

Dropping

As you lift your left hand, make the mental acknowledgement '**lifting**'. As you move the left forearm towards the body, say in mind '**moving towards**'. As the left hand is turned over, say in mind '**turning over**'. As the hand is moved downwards, say in mind '**dropping**', and as the hand is placed on the lap, say in mind '**setting down**'.

The same procedure holds for the left hand which is finally placed on the right hand. At this point you may wish to shift position to get comfortable. If so, make the mental acknowledgement **'getting comfortable'**. If you wear spectacles, remove them, place them on the floor and return your hand to the right position mindfully. Say in mind **'closing'** as you close your eyes. Then turn your mind inward, putting attention on the movements of the abdomen when breathing.

Sitting Meditation

When meditating, be aware of the rising and falling movements of the abdomen which accompany breathing. Focus attention on a point on the surface of the skin, about an inch (2cms) above the navel. Try to be aware only of the rising and falling of the abdomen, not the passage of the air through the nostrils or into and out of the lungs. Initially, if you find it difficult to fix attention on the movements of the abdomen, there are things you can do to be more aware of this area. Wearing a tight belt or rubbing a little balm on the spot above the navel, can make it easier to focus on the movements.

For the first sitting exercise, be mindful of the movement of the abdomen in two stages. When the abdomen rises, say in mind '**rising**' and when it falls, say in mind '**falling**'.

Don't try to control the movements, but be aware of them as they occur naturally. Try not to fall into a chant and lose track of the movements. If this happens, at the point where awareness returns, say in mind '**knowing; knowing; knowing**', and return your attention to the movements of the abdomen.

While practising Vipassana meditation, if a sound occurs, acknowledge in mind '**hearing; hearing; hearing**' and when the sound dies away, return the attention to the movement of the abdomen. If your attention 'follows' the sound, at the point that you become aware of what has happened, say in mind '**knowing; knowing; knowing**' and return your attention to the main object of meditation, the movement of the abdomen.

Similarly if there is a smell, acknowledge in mind '**smelling; smelling; smelling**'. If something is seen, either externally or internally, say in mind '**seeing; seeing; seeing**'. While tasting, acknowledge the taste '**tasting; tasting; tasting**'. When experiencing a cold, hot, soft or hard touch, acknowledge it in mind '**touching; touching; touching**'. Thinking is dealt with in the same way as the senses. It is not assigned greater importance. So while thinking, acknowledge in mind '**thinking; thinking; thinking**'.

If a feeling occurs, try not to be affected by it in any way, but simply acknowledge it as '**feeling; feeling; feeling**'. This remains the same whether the feeling is positive or negative, strong or weak. Try not to be drawn by any sensation, feeling or thought, but simply use 'mindfulness' or in other words 'bare awareness' to acknowledge whatever occurs.

Because some of the sensations that occur may be unfamiliar or very intense, it is easy to assign them greater importance than you do to everyday occurrences and so wish to stay with them, or to avoid them. Attempt to maintain equanimity and deal with all that occurs simply by acknowledgement, without prejudice or partiality, and then return your attention to the main object.

The length of the first sitting exercise is usually determined by the instructor, but the time is gradually increased as proficiency improves. Twenty minutes is usually sufficient for the first sessions. The timing does not have to be 'to the minute'. It is not necessary to use a stopwatch or alarm clock. Before starting an exercise, say in mind "I am going to meditate for twenty minutes", or whatever length of time you decide, and you will find that the timing will happen automatically.

Vipassana meditation is 'inclusive'. The exercises are intended gradually and systematically to build up concentration and energy levels through bare awareness of all that occurs in the present moment, so that the meditator may have direct experience of the ultimate truth or Nibbana.

How to Deal with Distractions

When practising walking, sitting or lying down meditation, if you hear a sound, be aware of it and say in mind '**hearing; hearing; hearing**', and then return to the main object of meditation. In walking, the main object is the movement of the feet. When standing, the main object is the position of the body. When sitting, it is the rising and falling movements of the abdomen etc.

Deal with other disturbances in the same way. Notice them with mindfulness and make appropriate mental acknowledgements. For example, while walking, you may start thinking about a problem at work. Try to catch the thought as it arises; don't think this is a good or a bad thought. Don't attempt to follow the thought to its logical conclusion; don't get angry with yourself for not being able to keep to the main object, but simply make the mental acknowledgement '**thinking; thinking; thinking**'. Then return your attention to the movement of the feet.

Suppose you are sitting and your leg starts to go numb. Don't move it. Instead, if you put your attention fully on the place where the numb feeling is occurring and say in mind '**feeling; feeling; feeling**', the sensation will probably diminish and may go away completely. If there is a feeling of pain, deal with it in the same way. Try not to move immediately, or to start thinking about the pain. Try not to ignore it; simply fix attention clearly on the place where pain is occurring and say in mind '**feeling; feeling; feeling**'. If after many acknowledgements the pain does not diminish and becomes unbearable, you may move; however,

45

you should do this mindfully. First say in mind '**intending to move**' three times. Then slowly and mindfully move to a new position, saying in mind '**moving; moving; moving**'. As a feeling of well-being or relief arises, say in mind '**feeling; feeling; feeling**' and return to the main object.

When meditating for a short time each day, really painful feelings do not usually develop. However, in a period of intense meditation, over a week or a month for example, the first few days are often extremely uncomfortable. This is quite natural, before concentration and mindfulness have built up to the optimum level. As you make further progress, the feeling of unbearable discomfort diminishes of its own accord.

The Second Walking Exercise

At the point when you can maintain bare awareness for the period set for walking meditation, without many distractions caused by a wandering mind, then you are ready for the second walking exercise.

In this exercise the meditator is mindful of the movement of each foot in two stages. As you lift the right foot, focus attention on that foot and make the mental acknowledgement 'lifting'. The foot should be lifted to about three inches (8cm) from the ground, trying not to show the sole of your foot to the person behind. Then slowly move the foot forward, keeping it at an even distance of three inches from the ground. No acknowledgement is made at this stage, but try to keep mindfulness on the movement of the foot. As the foot is lowered and touches

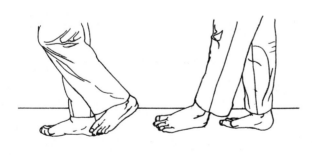

LIFTING   TREADING

the floor, say in mind '**treading**'. The process is identical for the left foot. In this exercise it is not necessary to make a distinction between right and left.

The first walking exercise may be practised for twenty to thirty minutes, followed by the second exercise for a further twenty to thirty minutes. However, if you are short of time, the period of time may be shortened. For example, if you can spare only forty minutes for meditation, you could spend ten minutes on the first walking exercise and ten minutes on the second, followed by twenty minutes of sitting meditation.

The Third Walking Exercise

In the third walking exercise the movement of the feet is divided into three stages. As the left or right foot is lifted, say in mind '**lifting**'. As the foot is moving forward, say in mind '**moving**' and, as the foot touches the floor, say in mind '**treading**'. To recap, the three stages of the third walking exercise are '**lifting; moving; treading**'. The instructions for standing, intending or wanting to walk at the start of the path, and for standing, intending to turn and turning at the far end of the path, remain the same as in the first exercise. Practise the first walking exercise '**left goes thus; right goes thus**' for 10 to 20 minutes. Then practise the second walking exercise '**lifting; treading**' for a further 10 to 20 minutes, followed by the third exercise '**lifting;**

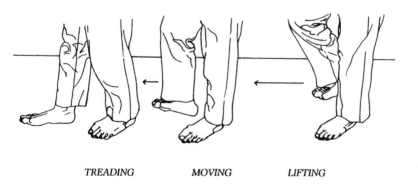

TREADING   *MOVING*   *LIFTING*

moving; treading' for 10 to 20 minutes. Then move mindfully into a sitting position. Remember that walking and sitting meditation exercises are alternated because they are mutually beneficial. The walking exercises help to increase energy and the sitting exercises help to increase concentration.

The Fourth Walking Exercise

The fourth walking exercise is as follows: As the left or right foot is lifted, be aware of the heel going up and say in mind '**heel up**'. Next focus attention on the lifting movement of the whole foot and say in mind '**lifting**'. As the foot moves forward, make the acknowledgement '**moving**' and as the foot touches the ground, acknowledge '**treading**'. Again, exercises 1 to 3 should each be practised for 10 minutes, before continuing to exercise 4 which should be practised for 10 to 20 minutes.

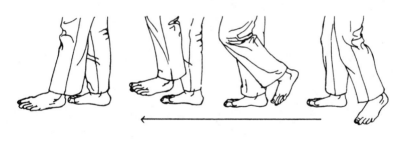

TREADING   MOVING   LIFTING   HEEL UP

TURNING IN THE FOURTH TO SIXTH WALKING EXERCISES

The walking exercises are designed to build up concentration and energy gradually. In the first exercise there is one stage of movement. In the second there are two stages and in the third, three. The first three walking exercises are designed to build up concentration, but the fourth marks a transition point. At this time you will usually begin to experience authentic insight knowledge. In this exercise the forward movement is divided into four stages and the awareness of turning is also refined. Instead of turning with four pairs of foot movements, the 180° turn is now made with eight pairs of foot movements. The angle of each section is approximately 22°; note that the right heel revolves on the same spot throughout.

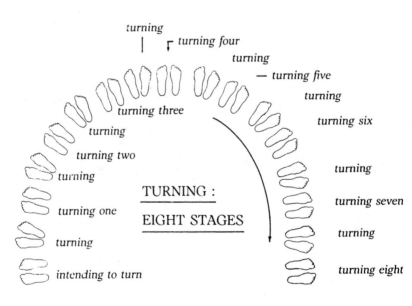

turning

turning four

turning

turning five

turning three

turning

turning six

turning

turning two

turning

TURNING :

turning

turning one

EIGHT STAGES

turning seven

turning

turning

intending to turn

turning eight

The Fifth Walking Exercise

The acknowledgements for the fifth walking exercise are '**heel up; lifting; moving; dropping; treading**'. In this case the downward movement of the foot is divided into two stages. Be aware of the downward movement before the foot makes contact with the floor as '**dropping**', and be aware of the foot making contact with the floor as '**treading**'. Remember to turn making eight pairs of foot movements. Exercises 1 to 4 are practised first, each for ten minutes, followed by the fifth exercise for 10 to 20 minutes.

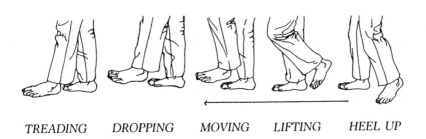

TREADING   *DROPPING*   *MOVING*   *LIFTING*   *HEEL UP*

The Sixth Walking Exercise

The sixth walking exercise has the following acknowledgements: **'heel up; lifting; moving; dropping; touching; pressing'**. After acknowledging the contact of the foot with the floor, focus awareness on the weight moving on to the foot as you move forward, simultaneously saying in mind **'pressing'**. There are eight pairs of foot movements when turning. Exercises 1 to 5 are practised first for 10 minutes each, followed by the sixth for 20 minutes. The complete sequence takes just over an hour.

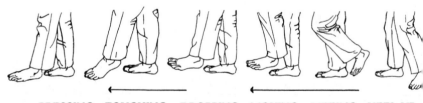

PRESSING   TOUCHING   DROPPING   MOVING   LIFTING   HEEL UP

Note: Your instructor will determine the point where you should progress from one walking exercise to the next. To recap, the acknowledgements for the six walking exercises are for all levels: **'standing; intending to walk'** followed by actual walking to the end of the space, then: **'standing; intending to turn; turning; standing; intending to walk'**.

For exercise one: 'left goes thus; right goes thus.'
For exercise two: 'lifting; treading.'
For exercise three: 'lifting; moving; treading.'
For exercise four: 'heel up; lifting; moving; treading.'
For exercise five: 'heel up; lifting; moving; dropping; treading.'
For exercise six: 'heel up; lifting; moving; dropping; touching; pressing.'

Walking meditation exercises are alternated with sitting exercises. The transition from walking to sitting should be made smoothly and mindfully. Be mindful of the intention to sit and of the actual sitting down movement. Try not to be distracted or to let your attention wander at this point.

Phra Debvedi writes, "In Vipassana, Sati focuses on the object and fastens it to the mind, or maintains the mind on the object. The aim is to use the mind as a place to lay the object down for examination and contemplation by the wisdom-faculty. One takes hold of the object in order to let wisdom investigate and analyse it, using the firm and stable mind as one's laboratory".[3]

The Second Sitting Exercise

The Ven. Phra Dhamma Theerarach Mahamuni, the late Chief Meditation Master of the Vipassana Centre at Section 5 Mahadhatu Monastery, in Bangkok, says in his book *The Path to Nibbana*, "After the performance of the mindful walking, begin to acknowledge the rise and fall of the abdomen in the sitting posture. In doing so, do not restrain the mind and body too much, or use too much effort. For example, there is a form of over-exertion which arises when one feels sleepy and tries to keep awake, or when one cannot acknowledge the constant changes in one's mind and body, but still keeps up the effort. One should also never be too slack in practice and allow the mind to act under the sway of various unhealthy tendencies whenever it has the inclination. One should practise according to one's capacity without too much restraint or effort, and without yielding to the power of latent tendencies. This is the 'Path of Moderation'."[5]

The instructions for the second sitting exercise are essentially the same as for the first. However, as concentration increases, a gap may be perceived after the abdomen falls and before it rises again. At this point you should put your attention on the sitting posture. This should be a nearly instantaneous sweep of mindfulness encompassing the act of sitting, followed immediately by mindfulness of the rising of the abdomen. The acknowledgements follow the sequence **'rising; falling; sitting'**.

RISING   FALLING   SITTING

The length of time spent on the second sitting exercise should be the same as spent on the current walking exercise. So, if the total time spent on the first three walking exercises is 40 minutes, then a further 40 minutes should be spent on the second sitting exercise. This is only a guide. The precise length of time will be determined by the instructor. Usually the third walking exercise and the second sitting exercise are introduced when you have experienced the first or second Vipassana *nana*, or level of Insight Knowledge.

The first Vipassana *nana* is characterised by the ability of the meditator to distinguish mentality *(nama)* from materiality *(rupa)*. In the second Vipassana *nana*, the meditator is able to perceive the conditioned inter-relationship between *nama* and *rupa*.

It is customary for the meditator to make regular reports to the instructor, who will generally ask questions to determine your progress. When he is satisfied that you have experienced the fifth, sixth or seventh Vipassana *nana* (level of Insight Knowledge), then the instructor introduces the fourth walking exercise: '**heel up; lifting; moving; treading**', followed by the third sitting exercise.

The Third Sitting Exercise

After your concentration has increased to enable you to be clearly aware of sitting, you will be asked to add a further acknowledgement 'touching'. At this point you are to bring your attention to all the parts of the body which are touching the floor. This acknowledgement continues from that of sitting. Attention is subsequently returned to the rising and falling of the abdomen. The sequence of acknowledgements is: 'rising; falling; sitting; touching'.

When it is clear that you have attained the eighth, ninth and tenth levels of Insight Knowledge, the fifth walking and the fourth sitting exercises may be introduced.

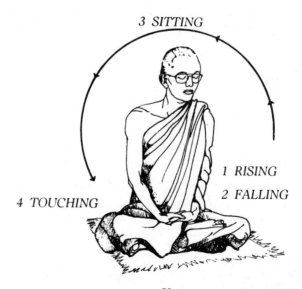

3 SITTING

1 RISING

2 FALLING

4 TOUCHING

More Complex Sitting Exercises

If you can already maintain good concentration, it may not be necessary to introduce the more complex sitting exercises. Also, children and older people may become confused and daunted by an expanded sequence of acknowledgements. However, if the fourth sitting exercise is introduced, the acknowledgement **'touching'** is further refined. You focus on the contact of the right buttock with the floor on one round, and then on the contact of the left buttock with the floor on the following round. The acknowledgments are **'rising; falling; sitting; touching'** (right buttock); **'rising; falling; sitting; touching'** (left buttock).

The third and fourth sitting exercises usually each last about one hour.

The fourth exercise may be further expanded as follows:

When you are able to keep attention clearly fixed on the points where your right and left buttocks touch the ground, you shift your attention to the knees.

At this stage of the exercise, you fix mindfulness on **'rising; falling; sitting; touching'** as before but, instead of being aware of the point where the buttocks are in contact with the ground, you mentally touch the right knee and, at the next cycle, the left knee:

'rising; falling; sitting' (making mental sweeping of the whole body)

'touching' (mentally touching the right knee)

'rising; falling; sitting' (mental sweeping of the whole body)

'touching' (mentally touching left knee).

TOUCHING   TOUCHING

RISING: FALLING: SITTING: TOUCHING (RIGHT KNEE)
RISING: FALLING: SITTING: TOUCHING (LEFT KNEE)

Perhaps, two or three days later, you may be asked to be aware of the right and left ankles, instead of the knees. There are finer subdivisions of attention, usually being aware of the parts of the body that are not touching the floor, but these will not be dealt with in detail here.

It should be borne in mind that the walking exercises mutually enhance the effectiveness of the sitting exercises and vice versa. They work together in tandem with the walking exercises helping to heighten energy levels, while part of the function of the sitting exercises is to build up concentration. Both energy and concentration are essential if Insight Knowledge (or *Vipassana nana*) is to develop.

Lying Down Meditation

You should remember that mindfulness should not be restricted to walking and sitting exercises. It should encompass all bodily functions and postures at all times. In fact, the meditator should try to maintain mindfulness (*Sati*) constantly. Lying down meditation further enhances awareness of all that occurs.

When moving into a lying down position, first be mindful of the intention to lie down, then be mindful of moving down and lying down, at the same time as the movements are occurring. As you start to bend down, you say in mind '**bending**'. As you move down, you make the acknowledgement '**going down**' or just '**down**'. As you touch the mat or mattress with your hands, '**touching**'. As other parts of the body touch the mat, '**touching**', and so on.

Just before going to bed is a good time to practise lying down meditation. With this you should be mindful of the movements of the abdomen, of the posture of lying down and of touching. The acknowledgements are '**rising; falling; lying; touching**'. You should be aware of the body touching the mattress or the floor.

As Dhanit Yupho has said, "In lying down meditation, it is advisable to meditate only before bedtime. . . . . . because, after lying down meditation, the meditator usually falls asleep".[6]

Bare Awareness

When asked to define the basic message of Buddhism, Buddhadasa Bhikkhu quoted a saying of the Buddha himself, "Nothing whatsoever should be grasped at or clung to".[4] When practising Insight meditation by noticing and acknowledging with bare awareness, we are simply using a method to train ourselves not to grasp nor cling to anything. It is not usually possible for a person whose whole life time has conditioned him to grasp and cling, to stop, simply because he realises it would be a good thing to do. The walking, sitting and lying down exercises are a systematic method to enable us to stop and, as the Buddha taught, "When seeing, just see. When hearing, just hear. When smelling an odour, just smell it. When tasting, just taste. When experiencing a tactile sensation, just experience it. When sensing a mental object, just sense it. Let things stop right there and insight will function automatically".

Many people ask, "Why do we have to keep making all these mental acknowledgements?" It is necessary to discipline and control the mind before we can bring about an optimum level of concentration. In Insight meditation the aim is neither forcefully to exclude sensations or thoughts, nor to repress them, but to see clearly how they arise, have being and pass away. A certain level of concentration and energy is necessary to keep them in our sphere of attention. Without this our minds jump all over the place, never attending fully to any one object. It is very difficult to stop your mind 'jumping around' simply by an effort of will. To slow down movements and make simple mental acknowledgements is a very effective tool to enable us to 'have stability, unshakeability and equilibrium', so that we are eventually able to — 'When seeing, just see. When hearing, just hear.'

In Vipassana meditation practice the ideal is constant mindfulness or bare awareness. 'Sati' is often translated as 'mindfulness', a term that can be misleading. The aim is quite the opposite of filling the mind with something. 'Bare awareness' is much closer. It is awareness without accompanying mental comment or emotional orientation. Another translation is 'heedfulness'. This is also preferable to 'mindfulness', because it carries the meaning of knowing what is happening at the time it is happening.

In Buddhism we talk about the Four Foundations of Mindfulness. The four are:
1. Mindfulness of the Body *(Kayanupassana)*,
2. Mindfulness of the Underlying State of Mind *(Cittanupassana)*,
3. Mindfulness of Feelings *(Vedananupassana)*,
4. Mindfulness of Mind Contents *(Dhammanupassana)*.

Mindfulness of the Body means in practice being aware of the position of the body at all times, but in particular when standing, sitting and lying down. It also means being heedful of the movements of the body.

Mindfulness of the Underlying State of Mind is the most difficult one of which to be aware. The meditator acknowledges the condition of mind at that moment. S/he notices if the mind is drowsy or alert, concentrated or distracted, clear or confused. It is rather like watching the glittering goldfish of thoughts and emotions swimming around in a bowl of water. Usually we notice the flash of gold, not the water in which the fish is swimming. *Cittanupassana* is being aware of the water (the underlying state of mind), not the fish of mental contents. Please note that this presupposes that awareness is not synonymous with the underlying state of mind. A confused or drowsy awareness would not be able to be clearly aware of itself.

In Buddhist psychology, consciousness is conceived of as an extraordinarily rapid set of successive mental instants. Each instant is neither separate from nor the same as the preceding one. One moment conditions the following one, but is not continuous with it. An analogy is often drawn to a mould which imprints a form on wax, but which is separate from it.

It is easier to be aware of **Mindfulness of Feelings** (*Vedananupassana*). By feelings is meant both sensations and emotions. Feeling hot or cold, and feeling happy or melancholic are part of '*Vedananupassana*'.

Feelings can be divided into three groups: pleasant, unpleasant and indifferent. When people start to meditate they are usually keenly aware of unpleasant feelings. Sitting still for any length of time makes us aware of unpleasant or even painful sensations in the body. Even if we sit on a comfortable chair without any constriction or strain, after a few minutes we usually wish to shift position.

If you observe people waiting at a bus stop, you will see they are constantly moving. They will shift their weight from one foot to the other, scratch their heads, rub their noses, cross and uncross their arms, put their hands in their pockets and take them out again. Even when waiting in a queue, we are constantly moving — but without awareness. If there is the slightest sensation of discomfort, the body automatically moves to try to counteract it.

In terms of meditation practice, unpleasant feelings are a great help to us, because they are so easy to be aware of. They demand our attention. We cannot ignore a painful sensation, whereas an indifferent one can easily pass unnoticed. Also very few people wish to prolong unpleasant, painful feelings, so there is a natural tendency to detach from them.

Pleasant feelings, however, beckon seductively. It is easy to become absorbed in them, to be drawn by them, simply because of their pleasant nature. We enjoy them and we want them to continue. If we have a feeling of happiness, we would like it to last for a long time; whereas, we would like a feeling of pain to go away as quickly as possible.

As with those people waiting at the bus stop, so many of our actions are really automatic reactions to changes in the environment. We are dancing to the tune of discomfort. The conductor is the desire for pleasure. But how often are we aware of the dance?

In Vipassana practice, meditators try to wake up to the dance. They deal with both pleasant and unpleasant feelings in the same way, by using 'bare awareness' or 'heedfulness'. Feelings of all types are allowed to enter awareness, are seen clearly, acknowledged and allowed to pass. However pleasant a feeling may be, it is not yet so transcendently pleasant as the sensation of a mind which rests in freedom.

There are also indifferent feelings. These are much more subtle. Meditators gradually become aware of these feelings as well. At the beginning of practice, we start by noticing those feelings which are conspicuous and easily perceptible. Gradually as energy and concentration increase, subtler sensations become evident. As practice continues, it is possible to catch sensations nearer and nearer their point of origin. However, at the beginning, we start with those sensations and feelings which can be easily noticed.

Sometimes several sensations may seem to appear at the same time. If awareness is not yet full, it may seem as though sensations can occur simultaneously. If this happens, simply acknowledge the feeling which is dominant at the instant. With acknowledgement, the sensation usually diminishes, allowing others to become apparent. Then succeeding sensations can be dealt with in the same way.

The fourth foundation of mindfulness is **Mindfulness of Mind Contents** (*Dhammanupassana*). In this group are included thoughts, daydreams, memories, projections of the future and so on. Buddhism talks of six senses: seeing, hearing, touching, tasting, smelling and the mind sense. The mind sense is not considered to be any more or less important than the other senses. The Western world admires the intellectual, the analyst and the planner. Intellectuals have become the aristocrats of popular favour in the late twentieth century.

Consequently, it is considered right to cultivate thought. Absent-minded professors can be found everywhere. Daydreaming schoolgirls drift along in a twilight zone of inattention to reality. Becoming lost in thought is a frequent occurrence.

If thoughts occur during meditation practice, like sensations and feelings, they are seen clearly, acknowledged and allowed to pass. Should a meditator become 'lost' in thought, he simply acknowledges '**thinking; thinking; thinking**' at the point where he becomes aware that he has been thinking. As we have been trained since childhood to cultivate thought, it will take some time to slow down the flow of thoughts. It is not necessary to reprimand yourself if thoughts seem to occur constantly.

The mind is, at any moment, a gift to us. Within the teeming flow of thoughts is the key to release. There is nothing wrong with thought per se. By the practice of '*Sati*' or 'bare awareness'; by letting the thought process occur in awareness and then allowing it to pass in awareness, a profound change begins to happen. Gradually thoughts occur less frequently. The space between distractions lengthens, and a sense of peace and freedom starts to arise.

So often, our awareness is not so much 'bare awareness', but a perception of the world veiled by preconceptions. The act of seeing, of registering a visual sensation, is almost always accompanied by a value judgment. If the object seen is pleasant, we orientate ourselves towards it. If the object is unpleasant a process of mental rejection occurs.

Consider spiders..... Some time ago I was staying in a meditation centre. It was late at night and I was lying down ready to go to sleep. When I looked across the floor to the corner of the room, I saw a large spider; a large, hairy spider; and as I looked at it, it seemed to grow larger, hairier and more fearsome.

I was filled with fear. I did not know if it was a poisonous spider or not. It just stood there poised and quivering. I was too scared to push it out of the door. So I just did nothing, watching the fear which was filling me. Eventually I fell asleep.

In the morning I went to have a closer look at where the spider had been. At that point there was a concrete step built up to stop water coming out of the bathroom and onto the wooden floor. The concrete was cracked, and these cracks combined with the gaps between the wooden planks of the floor, gave the appearance of a spider. There was no spider. It had been an illusion, but the fear had been as real as if it had been a real spider. We see the world in the same way. We live in fear and suffering because of our ignorance of the true nature of existence.

According to Buddhist philosophy, existence is a chain or cycle of inter-related events which constitute our experience of the world. It's a never-ending cycle or spiral, forever drawing us into the state of suffering or *Samsara*. The cycle of inter-relationships is called 'the Doctrine of Dependent Origination' or the *Paticcasamupada*. This is considered as a continuously revolving cycle. The sequence can be examined from any point in the cycle, but it usually written out as starting from the point of ignorance. Let me give you the sequence, starting from this point.

"Dependent on ignorance *(Avijja)*, there arise volitional activities *(Sankhara)*. From volitional activities there arises consciousness. Dependent upon consciousness, are mind and matter *(nama* and *rupa)*. From mind and matter there arise the six sense bases. Dependent upon the six sense bases, there arises contact. From contact arises feeling. Dependent upon feeling comes craving. From craving there arises attachment or clinging. Dependent upon attachment there arises becoming. From becoming there arises birth. Dependent upon birth are old age, death, sorrow, lamentation, pain, grief and despair".[7]

This cycle can be seen as a microcosm, as the process of our knowing the world at each passing moment, or it can be seen as a macrocosm, as the process of a human life.

Buddhism tells us how we can break out of the never-ending cycle of becoming and resultant suffering. It tells us precisely where to break that cycle, so that we can be truly free.

Remember the spider that was really just cracks in the floor of a darkened room? What was the reason for my fear? It was ignorance — ignorance of the true nature of the cracks. What is the cause of our feelings of unsatisfactoriness and suffering in life? Again, it is ignorance of life's true nature. This is the point at which we can break the ever-turning cycles of birth into pain and suffering. We can break the chain by knowing, really knowing the true nature of ourselves and of life. This is not theoretical knowledge, but experiential knowledge, gnosis or *Vipassana nana*. Perhaps it can be called the deepest wisdom, for it has the power to release us from the illusions that imprison our understanding.

There are three kinds of knowledge. The first is theoretical — remembering facts or learning them by heart like students in school. Then there is the knowledge gained by considering facts. Lastly, there is *Panna* or the wisdom gained by deep, experiential knowing. This third kind of knowledge can break the chain by destroying ignorance (*Avijja*).

Years ago, I attended a lecture by a Buddhist monk in a church hall in Hastings, a coastal town in the south of England. A glass of water had been placed on the lectern for the speaker. About half way through his speech, the monk paused. He slowly reached out, grasped the glass, carefully lifted it and mindfully sipped the water. Then equally slowly, the glass was lowered and placed on the wooden surface. Then the monk released his fingers from the cool glass and slowly and mindfully brought his hand back to rest on the papers on the lectern.

I do not remember one word from that speech, but the action of moving the glass with mindfulness had a profound effect on me. That was being awake. That was integration. That was really being alive.

The teacher may be your own child. Some years ago when my sons were quite young, they were asked to help to wash the dishes. In Thailand, as we are lucky enough to have a housegirl who usually does this chore, my sons were not used to washing dishes; however, on this occasion she was not there. They went into the kitchen and began. After sometime I began to realise how quiet it was in the kitchen. I think that most mothers would agree that quietness usually means something is amiss. So I sneaked a look through the door. Contrary to my expectation, the two boys were slowly, methodically and mindfully, washing and drying the dishes. They were quiet because they were concentrating on the task in hand. Wiping bubbles off a glass was done with awareness. They were really being there. Whereas I, the typical housewife, would usually wash the dishes on automatic pilot. Fast, yes. Efficient, yes. Aware, no.

How can we cultivate 'bare awareness'? You need to move slowly, carefully noting your movements. When you are walking, notice your movements at all times. Make acknowledgements. You can say '**right**' as your right foot moves; '**left**' as your left foot moves. '**Right; left.**' It is possible to continue practising mindfulness in this way. However, it often happens that when you are walking along the road and saying in mind '**right; left**', you suddenly find that you are saying '**right**' while the left foot is going down. Or you may be saying '**left**' when the right foot is going down. This shows that mindfulness has slipped.

When eating, be aware of picking up the spoon, lifting it, bringing it to your mouth. Be aware of the feeling of it coming into your mouth. Be aware of chewing. Be aware, if you can, of the movement of the food as it moves down into your stomach; some people can actually feel this.

When you are getting up or sitting down, at every point, notice what you are doing. Try to maintain mindfulness. As you prepare to lie down, notice the intention to lie down. Notice the movement as you put your hand down on the mattress. Be aware as you bend down, as your knees bend and touch the mattress. Be fully aware of all the component movements as you lie down. Try to be aware of everything that you do at all times. When you are having a wash, as you are drying yourself and getting dressed, as you are cleaning your teeth or going to the toilet — at all times, try to maintain mindfulness. Gradually, very gradually, as concentration and energy increase, you can develop the mind to a point where Insight comes up automatically.

The aim of Vipassana meditation is to reach Nibbana or enlightenment. This means the lightening of the heavy load of ignorance of the real nature of existence or a consummate insight into truth, and it can come at any moment. It is not dependent upon being in a certain position or being engaged in a prescribed activity.

There is the well-known story of the Venerable Ananda who was the attendant of the Lord Buddha. Some time after the passing away of the Lord Buddha, on the eve of the First Buddhist Council, Venerable Ananda was practising intensively because he had only reached the first level of enlightenment which is termed 'Stream Entry'; all the other members of the council were already *arahants*, that is, they had already reached full enlightenment. He had practised all night, but was unable to progress to the next level. He realised that he needed to balance concentration *(Samadhi)* with effort *(Viraya)*. He was about to change to the lying down posture. He had sat down and was just about to lie down, in fact, he was in position between sitting and lying down when he attained Arahantship at that instant. It is necessary to maintain constant mindfulness in order not to miss the potential message contained in each and every present moment.

The Five Hindrances

When we practise Insight meditation we are learning a new skill. In the same way as when we practise any new skill, at first we feel awkward. We feel uncertain of what we are doing. There may be some physical discomfort. There will certainly be some strain involved. We will meet resistance in ourselves.

It helps to have a strong motivation to practise. It helps to remind yourself of the reasons why you became interested in meditation. Why do people start to meditate?

Some come to practise through mental deliberation. They consider life around them. They study Buddhist texts and find in them convincing concepts. Then they wish to apply those concepts to their own lives. Others, through intellectual reasoning, come to see the limits of intellectual reasoning and so they wish to experience something which can transcend intellectual understanding without negating it.

Many people are dissatisfied with something in their lives, or experience boredom due to the repetitious nature of their working lives. Some are aware of a certain lack of depth in the pursuit of material possessions. Others have suffering in their lives. It may be physical suffering due to illness or unfavourable living conditions. For others the suffering may be mental or emotional. In the twentieth century most people who live in cities live tense, stress-filled lives; they wish to find a way out of suffering.

The Lord Buddha himself gave up his luxurious life as a prince when he became aware of suffering. He had led a protected life, shielded from all that was unpleasant. When he was born, Brahmin fortune tellers had predicted that the baby prince would either become a very powerful king or a Buddha.

His parents of course, wanted him to become a universal monarch. They tried to make the young prince's life as comfortable as possible so that he would not want to leave the worldly life. He was given three palaces in different parts of the country so that he wouldn't be troubled by changing seasonal conditions. He was surrounded by beautiful, young, healthy people. He married and he had a son.

When he was travelling outside the palace accompanied by his charioteer he saw, for the first time, an old man, then a sick man, a dead man and a meditating monk. These had a very profound effect on the sheltered young prince. He became intensely aware of suffering and he realised that all living beings were subject to it.

Later he contemplated that all qualities have their opposites. If there is heat there must be coldness. Whenever there is softness there must be hardness. If there is proximity there must be distance. Logically there must be an antithesis to the universal unsatisfactoriness and suffering inherent in life. This thought provided him with the impetus to leave his luxurious life at the palace and to search for that which is beyond suffering in all its myriad forms.

He was able to find the way to that state of ultimate release and to show it to others too, so that they could share that penultimate peace and bliss. His teaching continues to this day. It is carried on though the understanding and the example of the monks, nuns, laymen and laywomen.

Not everyone wants to meditate because he seeks the end of suffering. Some people come to meditation because they would like to experience exceptional states of mind. They would like to experience a heightened awareness. They would like to see glowing colours, to hear sounds from far away, or perhaps to re-experience the intensity of sensation dimly remembered from

early childhood. Such experiences may happen during the practise of Vipassana meditation, especially during intermediate levels of development, but not everyone has such experiences.

Some people come to meditation practice because they have
met someone who impressed them. Often these are gentle, calm
yet powerful people. Such people are good examples and others
would like to learn their secret. So if you feel that the practice is
too hard, remind yourself of the reason why you became interested in meditation and what is your aim, and this will increase
your patience and energy.

Now I would like to turn to more subtle problems that arise during meditation. They are termed the **Five Hindrances** or *Nirvarana*
in the Pali language. We wish to hold on to what we are familiar
with, especially our concept of ourselves. In the process of self-
discovery, which is part of Vipassana meditation, many of our
deep-seated ideas and feelings are called into question. Due to
this, your mind will find ways of avoiding deeper states of awareness. It puts up barriers to protect the self-image. These barriers
are termed hindrances. They are really tendencies of mind. Only
fully enlightened beings are free from hindrances. From time to
time, hindrances may arise in your meditation. However, they
can be overcome.

The first of the Five Hindrances, **sensual desire** *(Kamachanda)*,
is very subtle. Usually we do not even question the rightness of
seeking the pleasant and the comfortable. Twentieth century
life is built upon making ourselves as comfortable as possible.
Sensual desire anchors us to unsatisfactoriness *(Dukkha)*. As
soon as there is a state of wanting something, then by definition
something is not present. That moment is incomplete. It is without that which is desired. And even if we get gratification, it
cannot last, so there is the potential for unsatisfactoriness within
the moment of gratification. When we are young perhaps we
would like a tricycle to play with. Later we would like a bicycle,
later a smart, red sports car; later still a more luxurious model.

When we get what we want it gives but transitory satisfaction. Yet trying to get gratification, and the more refined the better, is considered normal.

One of the problems that meditators face is a wandering mind. When the mind gets carried along with thoughts, this is sensual desire too. It is much more pleasant and entertaining to let the mind wander or daydream, than to make the additional effort to be aware of the thinking process.

The second is **ill will** or *Byapada*. This encompasses all negative attitudes, both towards ourselves and others. This hindrance is much easier to deal with because it is painful and obvious.

Sleepiness or sloth (*Thina-middha*) is the third hindrance. Sleepiness and lack of energy occurs often during meditation practice. In sitting meditation the mind is not being constantly stimulated by sights and sounds and there is almost no physical movement, so it is easy to doze. Also the mind may be tired due to the effort expended trying to concentrate on one object of meditation for a long time.

It is not so easy to be aware of sleepiness. We may not be conscious of it at all until we wake up with a start. Try to be aware of drowsiness as soon as possible. If you mentally acknowledge the feeling '**sleepy; sleepy; sleepy**', the drowsy feeling will usually dissipate by itself. If the feeling of sleepiness continues, you can change to walking meditation to balance your energy and concentration. Also it is not advisable to sit for a long time when you begin to practise. There is no inherent advantage in sitting for long periods of time. A famous meditation master from Northeast Thailand, Ven. Ajahn Chaa used to say that hens can sit on their eggs for three days, but he had never met an enlightened hen. Ten minutes of walking meditation followed by ten minutes of sitting meditation is a suitable length of time for initial sessions.

Then there is **distraction and remorse.** The Pali '*Uddhacca-kukkucca*' is translated as flurry and worry, or as anxiety. Restlessness and worry are caused by thinking about the past and the future. We ask ourselves questions about an imagined future. Am I going to have enough money? Can I bring up my children well? Will I be healthy? We ask ourselves questions about a projection or a surmise. It is rather like crying at a sad movie. The trick is to try mentally to stay in the present moment. The past is just a memory and the future isn't here yet. What we can deal with is the present moment. We can really be aware of what is happening to us now.

The fifth hindrance is **doubt and uncertainty** (*Vicikicca*). Sceptical doubt is traditionally explained in this way: Was the Buddha really enlightened? Is the Dhamma really the truth? When we are sceptical we try to compare what we hear with what we already know. What we can know intellectually, that is, what we can put into words or conceptualise, is not on the same level as absolute truth. There can be no comparison, because we are comparing items from two different levels of experience.

Ayya Khema says *Dhamma* is beyond conceptualising. "Sceptical doubt tries to make a connection between limited concepts and the vastness of Dhammic understanding — it tries unsuccessfully. It feels bad."[8]

We need to loosen our perception from the limits of concepts and it is necessary to have faith to do this. We need '*Saddha*'. Saddha is not blind faith. It is the kind of faith which allows us to act, that empowers us. It is the kind of faith that we have in order to walk. We need to believe that the ground beneath our feet will not give way. If we see others who have confidence in the path, this will help us to have confidence too. If we see others walk across the ground, then we dare to follow. This is where the Good Friend (*Kalayanamitta*) is so invaluable.

Which would you prefer to follow? A map that was printed two thousand years ago or a guide who has made journeys through a mysterious foreign land? How do we know that he has really been there? He should be able to tell you clearly about the path. He should be able to tell you something about what you will see and hear on the way.

The Five Hindrances, sensual desire, irritation (ill will), sleepiness (sloth and idleness), worry, and distraction and doubt, arise due to a certain set of conditions. They are not our possessions. We are aware of them, but we do not need to feel that they are part of us like a hand or an arm. They arise when the requisite conditions are there, and then they go. If we have the right attitude to them and we know how to deal with them, they may go relatively quickly.

One of the dangers of travelling on the Bangkok buses is pickpockets. When I first arrived in Bangkok they took money from my bag several times. Then a friend told me how to avoid them. He said that when you get on a bus, you should look at the passengers who are near you. If you look straight at them, they know that you will be able to recognise them. They will know that you would be able to identify them, so they will think twice about stealing from you.

In the same way, we need to look straight at the hindrances that arise. We need to recognise them, face up to them and know them for what they are. In short, we need to acknowledge them. Then they will go away of their own accord.

You don't need to force them to go. The simple act of acknowledgement weakens their power. Avoidance or repression may allow a temporary hiatus, but pretending to yourself that you do not feel sleepy, for instance, will not help in the long run. It only causes delusion.

Let's look at another hindrance, ill will. It can be directed towards yourself or towards other people. Suppose you are practising sitting meditation and a feeling of pain arises. Many people experience pain in the legs. If you try to shut out the pain mentally, that is, ignore it, you may succeed temporarily, but then it will return more strongly than before. When this happens you may feel angry with yourself, because you cannot do a simple thing, like sitting still for a few minutes. Then there are two problems instead of one. There is the sensation of pain and there is the sense of anger towards yourself.

When a feeling of pain arises, we do not ignore it. Instead, awareness is placed on that point and it is acknowledged '**pain; pain; pain**', until it diminishes or goes away.

If you practise in a group, you may be disturbed by the other meditators. Someone may be breathing noisily. The thought may arise "That's not right. He should not disturb the others", or, "I should not allow myself to be disturbed by the sound. I'm a bad meditator". The whole sequence can be forestalled by the simple act of acknowledgement.

Expectation is a problem for experienced meditators. If they have had peaceful or uplifting experiences in the past, they may subconsciously wish to recapture them. In this case you may be comparing the experience of the present moment with the memory of the past experience. Expectation is just another feeling. When it arises, all you need to do is see it clearly, acknowledge it and let it go. It can be acknowledged as '**feeling; feeling; feeling**', or as '**hoping; hoping; hoping**'. Then the feeling will pass.

It will come and go like dark clouds in the sky. The sky remains boundless and clear. Your mind remains clear, undisturbed and open to the ever-new truth that is within each and every moment.

Impediments to Progress

When you start to make real progress and concentration has reached the optimum or 'access' level (*Upacara Samadhi*), which is a sustained form of concentration when the degree of attention enables you to be aware of the object's essential characteristics, many distractions may arise. These distractions take the form of strong emotions, sensations and fixed attitudes. They can be divided into ten groups and are referred to as '*Vipassana Kilesas*' or 'Defilements of Vipassana' meditation. It must be explained that it is attachment to the sensations that constitutes the defilement, not the sensations themselves.

Because these occurrences differ greatly from day-to-day experiences and are often very intense, you may sometimes become misled into believing that you have reached Nibbana already. In fact, you can view these experiences as signs that concentration has now reached an optimum level and feel encouraged. However, there should be no attachment to any pleasant sensations that arise. Conversely, there should be no avoidance of unpleasant sensations. Instead just let them come with mindfulness fully present and, as they change or fade away, similarly maintaining mindfulness, let them go.

Manifestations of Light (*Obhasa*) may occur. These may take the form of flashes of light like fireflies, beams of light, or perhaps rays of light which seem to be emitted from your heart and body. Alternatively, various complex, visual images may be seen; objects such as Buddha images or flowers may appear, or you may seem to gaze upon vast seascapes and so on. Sometimes the images, called '*Nimitr*', may be unpleasant or even frightening.

In all cases, deal with them in the same way. At the point where you become aware of 'light' or an image, you should say in mind **'seeing; seeing; seeing'** and allow the manifestation of light to fade away. Occasionally, more than three acknowledgements may be necessary. If an emotion arises as a result of the image, be clearly aware of the emotion at its inception and make the mental acknowledgement **'feeling; feeling; feeling'**. In this way you will be free of the control of the emotion, and so be able to make further progress.

The aim is neither avoidance nor repression of manifestations of light, or the emotions which may accompany them. 'Letting them come' is just as important as 'letting them go'. On the other hand, meditators are often fascinated by the supernatural quality of the images and light which start to occur at the third stage of Vipassana knowledge (*Sammasana Nana*). Consequently they wish to watch the gem-like brilliance and the apparently meaningful imagery for its own sake, seeking answers implied in the forms and the mystical strangeness. In this way, it is easy to become lost in a by-way. Because importance is assigned to the images, you may cling to them, or be carried along by them, watching an internal movie show. In this way defilement occurs because you can become attached to the imagery and be unwilling to let it go.

You may also experience feelings of joy or rapture (*Piti*). The Ven. Mahasi Sayadaw writes that rapture may produce "a sublime feeling of happiness and exhilaration, filling the whole body with an exceedingly sweet and subtle thrill".[9] Rapture is categorised into five states ranging from feelings of coolness and itching, to actual levitation. If you have become deeply absorbed into rapturous states, you may feel as if you are floating in a vast sea of joy, and your body may actually rise from the floor.

A novice monk from Wat Yai Chai Mongkol in Thailand's Ayuthaya province opened his eyes at the end of a meditation session to find himself sitting in a niche usually reserved for Buddha images, near the top of a chedi or stupa. He had to call to passers-by to bring ladders to enable him to get down. This is an extreme example of what can happen when a meditator fails to acknowledge the feeling of joy as it occurs, and so becomes controlled by it.

The feeling of rapture or joy is a gift and an encouragement and can be taken as a sign of progress. However, as with all sensations, pleasant or unpleasant, weak or seemingly powerful, familiar or exotic, rapture should be noticed with bare awareness, without partiality or prejudice. The meditator brings mindfulness clearly to the sensation and says in mind 'feeling; feeling; feeling'. In this way the feeling of joy still arises, but it does not become overwhelming and you can remain in peace.

Other 'Vipassana Kilesas' or Defilements of Vipassana meditation that can arise include 'Tranquillity of mental factors and consciousness' (Passadhi); Equanimity (Upekkha) and Mindfulness (Upatthana). As their names suggest, these are all admirable qualities which enable the meditator to observe all that occurs in the realm of materiality (rupa) and mentality (nama), with mental agility and a quiet, undisturbed mind. However, if you become attached to these states and believe that you have already reached the goal, these states too become corrupt. It is relatively easy to see the corrupting influence of, for example, a bloated spider image; but it is more difficult to observe the more subtle defilement of contentment arising from feelings of equanimity.

Another distraction that may occur is too much faith (Saddha). You may wish to persuade everyone to practise Vipassana. You may wish to perform meritorious deeds or build and repair Buddhist buildings and artifacts, or to give offerings to your teacher, or to continue practising for ever. One lady meditator went to pay respect to the Buddha by lighting incense and candles, many, many times throughout the day. If a ceremony was being conducted she would walk through the ceremony seemingly oblivious to it, in order to light incense in front of the Buddha image. Her emotional faith had become so strong that she was no longer aware of the present moment.

Very sublime feelings of happiness (*Sukha*) may arise. Bliss or happiness may vary in intensity from a feeling of comfort to a wish to keep practising for a long time, due to pleasant feelings.

Exertion (*Paggaha*) is another impediment that can occur, causing the meditator to practise too strenuously. You may over-exert yourself, so that your attentiveness and clear-conscious-ness become weak causing distraction and lack of concentra-tion. Or at this stage, too, you may become attached to the fact that energy and concentration have now reached a state of equi-librium. This state of equilibrium enables energy to act evenly, and you may find that you are able to overcome agitation and sleepiness. Whatever occurs in the present moment you will notice keenly and continuously. It is very easy to wish to stay in this state. The very act of wishing it to stay already disturbs the balance and may inhibit further progress.

Another thing which may happen is that you may become distracted by 'thoughts' about meditation. You may consider various principles which you know or have studied. You may misunderstand, but think that you are right and want to contest your teacher. Alternatively you may become attached to the fact that your awareness has become very keen and lucid.

The ten groups are :

1.   Manifestations of light or illumination (*Obhasa*)
2.   Joy or rapture (*Piti*)
3.   Tranquillity (*Passadhi*)
4.   Bliss (*Sukha*)
5.   Faith or religious fervour (*Saddha*)
6.   Exertion (*Paggaha*)
7.   Mindfulness (*Upatthana*)
8.   Knowledge (*Nana*)
9.   Equanimity (*Upekkha*)
10. Gratification or satisfaction (*Nikanti*)

Feelings of rapture, great faith or images *(Nimitr)* may occur at any stage after access concentration has been reached. However at later stages you will have become relatively skilled at coping with them. When they first arise — you can easily become misled into assigning them greater importance than they deserve. Because they are unfamiliar and intense, you could become overly fascinated or frightened.

Sometimes your body may shake uncontrollably. There may be nausea, actual vomiting, diarrhoea or excessive perspiration. The latter are signs that purification or cleansing is taking place. As your meditation deepens further, they will cease of their own accord.

There may be feelings of heat or coolness. The body may seem to expand or contract or lean over. All are signs that concentration has reached optimum level and they should be dealt with by maintaining bare awareness and making appropriate mental acknowledgements. In this way you can go on to deeper states of awareness and insight.

The Three Marks of Existence

As we practise meditation, and in particular Insight meditation, we go through many levels of experience and ever-deepening levels of understanding.

Gradually we become aware of the Three Characteristics, or Marks, of Existence. We experience them with new clarity. Indeed, the contemplation of any one of them may well constitute the trigger condition for insight to arise. The Three Characteristics, or Marks, of Existence, are termed in Pali the *Tilakkhana*. *Ti* means three; *lakkhana* means the fundamental characteristics of phenomenal existence. These three marks characterise all animate organisms and inanimate objects in the universe.

The three characteristics are:

1. *Anicca* which can be translated as impermanence or transience.
2. *Dukkha* which is usually translated as suffering, but which is more accurately rendered as unsatisfactoriness.
3. *Anatta* or non-self. These words 'Anicca', 'Dukkha' and 'Anatta' signify the characteristics of every facet of life, mental or material. They are interrelated.

The Buddha said "Everything is transient. Everything which is transient is unsatisfactory. Everything which is transient and unsatisfactory is not self." Usually the characteristics of unsatisfactoriness (*Dukkha*) and impermanence (*Anicca*) are more easily comprehended. But it is the third, non-self (*Anatta*), which is uniquely Buddhist. It is often necessary to come to an

84

understanding of 'Anatta' through unsatisfactoriness and impermanence.

In fact, when deep realisation occurs, the nature of these three
characteristics will be revealed simultaneously, although any one
of them may be dominant or may be the key to unlock the barriers of ignorance.

'Dukkha', or unsatisfactoriness, is within our range of awareness at all times, but we are adept at avoiding noticing it in its
subtler forms. We usually consciously register unsatisfactoriness
when it becomes intense enough to be felt as pain or suffering.
'Dukkha' may be mental or physical suffering. When you watch
people, most of them constantly shift their position. As soon as
there is the slightest discomfort they will move. The movement
brings temporary relief. But a few seconds later another form of
discomfort will arise, resulting in another movement. In the same
way, our attention will be shifting ceaselessly from object to
object, seeking amusement or avoiding boredom and distress.
Dukkha encompasses a whole range of feelings, from mild irritation to deepest anguish.

Buddhism does not deny that there can be happiness in life.
However, the teachings point out that whenever there is happiness, we would like to hold on to it. We wish it to continue, to
last. But unfortunately the second characteristic of existence
— 'transitoriness' or 'impermanence' (Anicca), always manifests
itself. Even the most ecstatic moments of happiness cannot last
for ever. 'Dukkha', or suffering, arises when we try to hold on to
happiness. We strive in vain to prolong bliss, because the very
nature of all conditioned things is a constant flux and change.

We can see examples of impermanence all around us. The
differences among them lie only in the length of change. We
can observe the changing quality of light through the day. The
seasons change from cool to hot, and back again. They change
from wet to dry. A tiny bud swells to become a lovely flower
which then withers and fades. A child outgrows his clothes. The
face in the mirror changes imperceptibly, day by day. Trees may

live for hundreds of years, but they too die eventually. Stones erode to sand. Whole continents shift. The light of our sun has already dimmed from white to yellow. Later it will fade to orange and then dull red. Then it will no longer be able to sustain life on this planet. The whole universe is in motion, expanding here, contracting there; it is also breathing.

Ego tends to believe that it is immortal, that it can last for ever. But if you think of how you have changed since you were a baby, a toddler, a child, you can see that it is not only the body that undergoes change. Personality changes too. We are moulded by our experiences and by the way in which we react to them.

The longer cycles of change can be grasped by the intellect, but it is not until we become aware of the shorter, in fact, virtually instantaneous cycles of change within our living experience of being, that impermanence begins to be really known.

Is the hand which rested on your knee a moment ago the same as the one now on the desk? When your concentration is one-pointed and even, when mindfulness is full, then you will know the answer to that question — not by analogy or surmise, but by direct experience.

During Vipassana meditation we are both the observer and the observed. As we come to experience impermanence in our own bodies and minds, then we can come to know non-self ('Anatta'). Buddhism does not deny that there is a physical body, and mentality. It does not deny the existence of this combination of materiality/mentality. Quite the opposite, a meditator uses the mind/body complex as the object of meditation. What Buddhism refutes is the existence of a permanent, unchanging entity called self.

For practical, everyday purposes, in order to sustain life, it is necessary to identify with the body and mind to some extent. Buddhism discourages us from clinging to this entity, because when we cling to that which is unstable, we will fall, causing suffering to arise. Our view of self is rather like a cube of ice. It is frozen into what seems like form with apparent characteristics and distinguishing marks. But when we cling to the ice cube, it melts. It runs out between our fingers. Its fluidity, its changing nature become apparent. However hard we try, we cannot hold on to the momentary solidity born of conditions.

As we meditate in a state of mindfulness, we gradually build up both energy and concentration in balance, until our minds become finely tuned, clear, free from expectations, bias and prejudice. In this state of mind, the three characteristics become apparent. We experience them in this very moment, not as an intellectual concept, and not as blind belief, but as actual experience.

Mind can become still, unshaken by external or internal disturbances. It can become like a mountain which is undisturbed by the storms raging around it. The mountain represents the still mind, not caught up in habitual reactions to the environment. Such a mind is not making judgments about what is good or bad according to a concept of what is or is not beneficial to self.

In Vipassana the mind is stilled, not because the winds of sensation, emotion and thought are absent, but because the source of agitation is clearly seen. When this is seen clearly, it ceases by itself.

We cannot 'get' or 'attain' enlightenment. Enlightenment constitutes a letting go, a release from the burden of a sense of self. With the clear-seeing wisdom born of direct experience, we can let the concept of self go, so that enlightenment 'is'. The three keys to enlightenment are here in every moment. They are not hidden; we only need to open our awareness to them. Unsatisfactoriness (*Dukkha*), impermanence (*Anicca*) and non-self (*Anatta*), when directly experienced, can unlock the barrier of ignorance and allow enlightenment 'to be'.

"Though one may live a hundred years with no true insight or self-control, yet better indeed, is a life of one day, for a man who meditates in wisdom."[10]

The Benefits of Vipassana Meditation

The benefits of Vipassana meditation range from increasing your ability to cope with day to day problems, to the experience of profound peace that results from the ultimate release of tensions. This takes place when the nature of existence is fully experienced and known. It is a truism that each of us is different. In the practise of Vipassana as in all else, the time taken to gain benefits varies. But, even if we cannot become an enlightened being (*Arahant*) immediately, everyone can benefit in some way.

The simple expedient of stepping back from the immediate involvement that results from sense input, allows the meditator a split second in which to choose to react or not. In practice this means that angry reactions can be better controlled. Problems which used to appear overwhelming and unsolvable come to be seen in a different light. You will become more capable and unruffled, which has obvious advantages both in the office and at home. The housewife who arranges her day to include half an hour or forty minutes of the tension-unravelling provided by Vipassana meditation is less likely to shout at the children or to feel unbearably tired and depressed. The businessman who refuses a liquid lunch with friends, locks the door of his office, and takes half an hour to calm and clear his mind, is more likely to make the right decisions, even under pressure. He is unlikely to be manoeuvred by associates who seek to flatter or deceive in order to further their own ends, because he will be clear-minded enough to be aware of what is happening.

It is the nature of existence that everything changes. Sometimes it may be possible to move smoothly and effortlessly into deep states of awareness, while at other times it may be difficult to sustain concentration for even a few moments. Setting aside a regular time for daily practice will help. If we practise at approximately the same time each day, we get used to it and we become ready for the practice. It is rather like waking up before the alarm clock rings.

Other benefits of Vipassana meditation include improved health. Diseases which are exacerbated by tension show real improvement, such as high blood pressure, migraine and some forms of paralysis. A famous meditation instructor, Goengar, suffered from migraine for many years. He had travelled to many countries unsuccessfully seeking a cure. He found relief after practising Vipassana for a short time.

You may, then, seem to age less quickly than your peers. The deep peace and energy from within radiate out, so that, especially during intensive periods of meditation, your appearance will change. As tensions are released from within, your posture relaxes, movements become more fluid and youthful. The skin texture may change and your face may glow with an inner light. The change in external appearance mirrors internal changes. Having experienced clear-seeing, untainted by bias or prejudice, we realise that we have been walking around half-blind.

The advantages of meditation can be seen in three different ways: advantages which can be obtained in the present life (Ditthadhammikatta), e.g. changes in appearance or relief from certain illnesses; advantages which can be obtained in future lives (Samparayikatta); advantages on the highest, supramundane level (Paramattha).

All actions have a result which may not be immediately apparent. There may be a delayed reaction, but eventually there will be a result. If we train our minds, a positive action will eventually have a positive result. Buddhists believe that the result may occur in a future life.

The highest advantages, the supramundane advantages, concern the attainment of the four stages of the path, culminating in the end of suffering and accompanied by the realisation of perfect bliss.

The deepest benefit occurs when, through wisdom, we are able to stop grasping and clinging to the sense of self. Feelings of tranquillity and rapture come and go, but the deepest knowledge is all-pervading and outside time. In Vipassana meditation the aim is freedom, freedom from the burden of suffering. It is gained through insight wisdom. As mindfulness and concentration develop in a state of balance and if there is enough energy and clear comprehension (Sampajanna), then insight wisdom can arise.

In Vipassana you will clearly perceive all that occurs in the present moment. Because you are not attached to anything, it is possible to be aware of the deepest tendencies within. You can know the roots of attachment and aversion, and eradicate these tendencies at the point where they originate.

The type of benefit depends on the strength of practice and the maturity of the individual. But all who sincerely attempt to follow the path will obtain a positive result. One person may progress more slowly than another. Buddhists believe that this is due to the amount of merit (a store of as yet unmanifested good results) acquired in the past. The person who makes rapid progress is thought to be reaping the result of previous good actions.

As soon as we start to meditate we come to realise that this mind, which we thought was controllable and lucid is, in fact, restless, vacillating and difficult to control or restrain.

A verse from the Dhammapada says:
"Mind foreruns all mental conditions.
Mind is the chief, mind-made are they,
If one speaks or acts with a pure mind,
then happiness follows one
even as a shadow that never leaves."

So if we can calm and restrain the mind, benefits are sure to arise. Looking again at the benefits which can occur in this life, one who is practised at dealing with negative emotions such as boredom, anger, revulsion, irritation or fear during meditation, will carry some of that approach over into family life or any other social interaction. Being mindful and mentally noting the arising of such emotions works in everyday life too. The frustration that arises when you are caught in a traffic jam, or the exasperation that comes when you have to deal with a lazy co-worker can be dealt with in the same way as a painful sensation that arises during meditation.

Instead of ignoring the feeling, diverting our attention or kicking the cat, we simply watch the sensation or emotion as it arises, see it clearly, acknowledge it and watch it as it passes. Being aware enough to catch the beginning of an emotional reaction is dependent upon bare awareness (*Sati*). If this can be maintained, little energy is lost through heedless, emotional reactions. That energy is then available for positive use.

Imagine you are holding a bowl which is completely full of water. If you walk along with concentrated attention, very little water will spill. But if you walk along with jerky, uncontrolled movements, a lot of water will be lost. In the same way, if we walk through our daily tasks and social interactions with mindfulness, little energy will be needlessly lost.

Social interaction becomes smoother for the mindful person. Anger and other negative emotions no longer control you. At the very least they are reduced. You gain the friendship and respect of those with whom you live and work. People feel happy to be near you. You will not feel afraid to tell the truth about the situation. So decisions can be made on valid information. Such decisions are more likely to produce the results you desire.

If we are clearly aware of what we are doing at the point of doing it, we can avoid many unnecessary checks and repetitions. So often we act on 'automatic pilot' when we cannot remember what we have done. We have to go back and check again. For example, if you are in a hurry to go to work, you might leave the house, lock the door and walk half way down the path, and then suddenly wonder if you remembered to lock the door or not. So you have to turn round, go back and check the door and then start out again. If the original action had been done mindfully, no such checking would have been necessary.

The relaxed, peaceful states which accompany a one-pointed mind are like a mental holiday. Afterwards, the relaxed mind is better able to cope with the problems of the day. Experienced meditators say that if they miss daily practice it feels as if they have forgotten to have a bath.

As the ability to concentrate increases, it can be used effectively in work situations. Attention can be fixed on the task in hand and stay with it until the job is done. Work gets done faster and with fewer mistakes. Because the work is done more efficiently, more time then becomes available for formal meditation and so the positive cycle continues.

You may experience heightened states of awareness. As your mind cools and calms down, your awareness of the immediate surroundings will increase. Your senses will become more acute. The experience of the moment will become fresh and immediate. There is a reintegration into being fully alive. Your sense of sight becomes refined, colours glow with extraordinary intensity. They seem to be lit from within. Minute details become apparent, to the extent of being able to see the scales on a butterfly's wings or each individual hair on the back of your hand. The awareness of sounds and textures becomes far more acute, and the scents and odours of childhood return.

Side effects of the development of concentration may happen to some people. Some develop powers of telepathy, clairaudience and clairvoyance. While these abilities are certainly extraordinary, they should not be thought of as the highest aim of meditation. The highest aim is to develop Insight. There are sixteen levels of Insight Knowledge. These are termed 'Nanas', and are almost always accompanied by deep states of absorption.

The process of unravelling attachment through actual experience, although different for each individual, also has certain common characteristics. At first the meditator comes to know mentality/materiality (*nama rupa*). Mentality is that which names. Materiality is form, or that which can be named. As insight develops you will come to see how they are inter-related. Concentration deepens and the 'Defilements of Insight' may arise. These distractions have a fascination all of their own. Beautiful or ugly visions may occur. You may feel as if you are flying or floating in a sea of light. Great waves of happiness may seduce you into believing that you are already enlightened.

While these wonderful experiences are certainly a sign of progress, they do not constitute enlightenment. As you continue to practise, you will come to see the endings of processes, feelings, thoughts and sensations. Following an acceptance of the transitory nature of all things, a loosening of attachment to those things occurs. There may be a stage of disillusionment. You will then become aware of the fearful nature of the changing, unsatisfactory world. Then the desire arises to be released from the prison of attachment to the shifting mire of conditioned existence. Later, composed clear-seeing may arise. At this point if the meditator has acquired enough merit, there may be a leap beyond to a 'supramundane' level where awareness has Nibbana as its object. When this happens the defilements which have been causing suffering are eradicated at the root. The Stream of Enlightenment has been entered.

The Four Foundations of Mindfulness (*Satipatthana*) are considered to incorporate both Samatha (Calmness) meditation and Vipassana (Insight) meditation. Combining the concentration built up through Samatha meditation with the wisdom developed in Vipasssana meditation is the way to real freedom.

In the "Mahasatipatthana Sutta", the Buddha said of the foundations of mindfulness:

"This is the one way, O Bhikkhus, for the purification of

beings, for the passing beyond sorrow and lamentation, for the cessation of pain and distress, for the attainment of the supramundane path, for the realisation of Nibbana".

Some Notes about Practice

Although it is not essential to follow an organised group course or the precise method of practice described here, it is very helpful to have a 'Good Friend' or guide, especially when starting Vipassana practice. It is not necessary to be a Buddhist to make use of this method of mind development. Indeed you don't need to know that this is a Buddhist method of meditation. The Buddha himself said that there are some who, though they had not heard the *Dhamma* directly from him, would still be able to walk the right path. "There were some who, not having heard it from the Buddha, through continuous reflection, consideration and study, through constant observation and practice, would nevertheless be able to walk the right path."

Vipassana meditation is suitable for all men, women, children, old and young alike. Lay people, as well as monks and nuns, can practise. This book is intended as a guide, a practical guide to the more organised systems of Vipassana practice. However, meditators are strongly advised to have some first-hand guidance to start with.

The Noble Eightfold Path

Meditation in all its forms is included in the Noble Eightfold Path. A person will not be able to meditate successfully if his lifestyle is not conducive to the practice. The Noble Eightfold Path is the way that leads to the extinction of suffering. It is divided into three main groups. Morality *(Sila)*, Concentration *(Samadhi)* and Wisdom *(Panna)*.

The first group: '**Morality**' comprises
Right speech *(Samma Vaca)*
Right action *(Samma Kammanta)* and
Right livelihood *(Samma Ajiva)*
The second group: '**Concentration**' comprises
Right effort *(Samma Vayama)*
Right mindfulness *(Samma Sati)* and
Right concentration *(Samma Samadhi)*
The third group: '**Wisdom**' is composed of
Right understanding *(Samma Ditti)* and
Right view on thought *(Samma Sankappa)*.
Let me describe these in more detail quoting Ven. Dr. H. Saddhatissa:

(1) **Right Understanding:**
To begin treading the Path we must see life as it is, in accordance with its three characteristics of impermanence, suffering and self-lessness; we must possess a clear understanding of the nature of existence, of the moral law, of the factors and component elements

which go to make up the continuing round of birth and death.

(2) Right Thought:

This means that our mind should be pure, free from sensory desire, ill-will, cruelty and the like. At the same time, we should be willing to relinquish anything that obstructs our mental and psychological progress.

(3) Right Speech:

Correct speech should not be unduly loud or excitable, not prompted by prejudices, ill-will or selfish interests. It should not be such as to inflame passions or arouse the emotions.

(4) Right Action:

This generally consists of observing the Five Precepts, which can be shown in both their positive and negative aspects:
1. Not to kill, but to practise love and harmlessness to all,
2. Not to take that which is not given, but to practise charity and generosity,
3. Not to misuse the senses, but to practise purity and self-control,
4. Not to indulge in wrong speech, but to practise sincerity and honesty,
5. Not to participate in taking any intoxicating drinks or drugs which cause heedlessness, but to practise restraint and mindfulness. For the ordinary disciple, moreover, it is essential to practise all these injunctions if he wishes to aspire to the higher life.

(5) Right Livelihood or Vocation:

The layman should only pursue an occupation that does not cause harm or injustice to other beings. He should have a sense of service and duty in life.

(6) Right Effort:

Self-perfection can be achieved by avoiding and rejecting unhealthy qualities while acquiring and fostering skillful qualities. This stage is subdivided into four parts:

a. The effort to prevent the arising of unskilled thoughts, words and deeds which have not yet arisen.

b. The effort to expel that unskill which has already been and which is present.

c. The effort to induce healthy thoughts, words and actions.

d. The effort to cultivate all the good words, thoughts and actions which are already present.

(7) Right Mindfulness:

This implies a state of constant awareness with regard to the body, feelings, mind, and the ideas that are created by it. Mind, according to Buddhism, is the sixth sense and nothing more. The development of this type of mindfulness is necessary to enable the meditator not to be led astray by wrong thinking.

(8) Right Concentration:

At the final stage, we should aim at one-pointedness of mind directed towards a wholesome object. To do this, we should sit quietly, with a tranquil mind and, if wandering thoughts arise, patiently discipline the mind anew, stopping and expelling them. Breathe naturally. Breathing must not be controlled or interfered with in any way, otherwise it is impossible to understand the important signs that the breaths show. Devices, like counting, are usually necessary at first to ensure concentration and absorption, but can be discarded once we have mastery of our minds, and can prevent them from wandering away from the task in hand. [11]

Sources of Quotations

1. Christmas Humphreys - quoted in *Zen to Go* by Jon Winokur. New American Library, 1988, New York.

2. Robert Linssen - *Living Zen.* Trans. by Diana Abrahams Cariel. Grove Press, 1958, New York.

3. Debvedi - *Sammasati: Right Mindfulness.* Trans. by Dhamma-Vijaya. Amarin Printing Group, 1988, Bangkok.

4. Buddhadasa Bhikhu - *Handbook for Mankind.*

5. Ven. Phra Dhamma Theerarach Mahamuni - *The Path to Nibbana.* Trans. by Vorasak & Helen Jandamit. Vipassana Centre Sec. 5, Mahadhatu Monastery, 1988.

6. Yupho - *Self-Study: Practical Insight Meditation.* The Dharmanoon Singgaravanij Foundation; Siva Phorn Limited Partnership, 1984.

7. Ven. Jagararo - *Introduction to Meditation.* Bodinyana Monastery, Perth, Australia.

8. Ayya Khema - *Being Nobody, Going Nowhere.* Wisdom Publications, 1987, Boston, Mass., U.S.A.

9. Ven. Mahasi Sayadaw - *The Progress of Insight.* Trans. by Nyanaponika Thera. Buddhist Publication Society, 1978.

10. *The Dhammapada.*

11. Ven. Dr. H. Saddhatissa - *A Buddhist's Manual.* Kowah Printing and Publishing Co., 1976.

GLOSSARY

Anatta: One of the Three Marks of Existence: non-self, insubstantiality, uncontrollability.

Anicca: Impermanence, one of the Three Marks of Existence.

Anussatis: Recollections - a group of six meditation devices.

Arahant *(Pali)*, **Arhat** *(Skt)*: An enlightened being - one whose mind is free from mental obsessions.

Asubha: A meditation device used to reduce attachment to the physical body, e.g. a skeleton or a corpse.

Avijja: Ignorance.

Bhagavan: The Awakened One.

Bhavana: Mental culture.

Brahmaviharas: Excellent qualities - a group of four meditation objects comprising Loving Kindness *(Metta)*; Compassion *(Karuna)*; Sympathetic Joy *(Mudita)* and Equanimity *(Upekkha)*.

Byapada: Ill will - one of the Five Hindrances.

Cattari Ariya Saccani: The Four Noble Truths.

Cittanupassana: One of the Four Foundations of Mindfulness - Mindfulness of the Underlying State of Mind.

Dhamma *(Pali)*, **Dharma** *(Skt)*: The truth within the teachings of the Lord Buddha or, alternatively, the texts which contain that truth. The deepest Truth.

Dhammanupassana: One of the Four Foundations of Mindfulness - Mindfulness of Mind Contents.

Ditthadhammikatta: Advantages which can be obtain in the present life.

Dukkha *(Pali)*, **Duhkha** *(Skt)*: Unsatisfactoriness, suffering. The First Noble Truth and one of the Three Marks of Existence.

Iriyapatha *(Pali)*: Positions and postures of the body, especially during meditation.

Jhana *(Pali)*, **Jnana** *(Skt)*: Absorption, trance - a state of serene contemplation attained by meditation.

Kalyanamitta: A Good Friend.

Kamachanda: Sensual desire - one of the Five Hindrances.

Kamma: Action or deed and its result.

Kasina: A meditation device. A (usually) circular object used in Samatha meditation as a means to develop concentration. There are ten kasinas: earth, water, fire, air, red, blue, yellow, white, space and light.

Kayanupassana: One of the Four Foundations of Mindfulness - Mindfulness of the Body.

Khanika samadhi: Momentary concentration.

Kilesas *(Pali)*, **Klesas** *(Skt)*: Defilements, impurities, impairments.

Magga *(Pali)*, **Marga** *(Skt)*: The Fourth Noble Truth. The Way leading to the Cessation of Suffering.

Mahamuni: Great Teacher.

Majjhima Patipada: The Middle Way.

Metta: Loving Kindness - one of the four Brahmaviharas.

Nama: Mentality - that which knows materiality.

Nana: Wisdom, level of Insight knowledge.

Nibbana *(Pali)*, **Nirvana** *(Skt)*: Enlightenment.

Nikanti: Gratification.

Nimitr: Mental images seen in meditation.

Nirodha: The Third Noble Truth - the Cessation of Suffering.

Nirvarana *(Pali)*: The Five Hindrances.

Obhasa: Manifestations of light - one of the defilements of Vipassana meditation.

Paggaha: Exertion - one of the defilements of Vipassana meditation.

Panna: Wisdom.

Paramattha: Advantages of the highest (supramundane) level.

Parinibbana *(Pali)*, **Parinirvana** *(Skt)*: The passing away of the Lord Buddha.

Passadhi: One of the defilements of Vipassana - tranquillity of mental factors and consciousness.

Paticcasamupada: The Doctrine of Dependent Origination.

Piti: Joy, rapture - one of the defilements of Vipassana meditation.

Ratanattaya: The Triple Gem - the Buddha, the Dhamma and the Sangha.

Rupa: Materiality.

Saddha: Faith.

Samadhi: Concentration.

Samatha: Concentration meditation, also called calmness or tranquillity meditation.

Samma Ajiva: Right livelihood.

Samma Ditti: Right understanding.

Samma Kammanta: Right action.

Samma Samadhi: Right concentration.

Samma Sankappa: Right thought.

Samma Sati: Right mindfulness.

Samma Vaca: Right speech.

Samma Vayama: Right effort.

Sammasana Nana: Knowledge of comprehending mentality/materiality as unsatisfactory and not-self.

Sampajanna: Clear comprehension.

Samparayikatta: Advantages that can be obtained in future lives.

Samsara: The cycle of continuity. The beginningless cycles of birth and death.

Samudaya: The Second Noble Truth - the Origin of Dukkha.

Sangha *(Pali)*, **Samgha** *(Skt)*: 1. Spiritual community, 2. The ordained community of monks and nuns and 3. The community of those who have attained some degree of awakening.

Sankhara: Volitional activities.

Sati: Mindfulness, bare awareness, heedfulness.

Satipatthana Vipassana: Vipassana meditation which is based on the Four Foundations of Mindfulness.

Sila: Morality, ethical conduct.

Sukha: Happiness.

Tatiyajhana: The third *Jhana* (absorption).

Thina-middha: Sloth and torpor, sleepiness - one of the Five Hindrances.

Tilakkhana: The Three Marks of Existence - unsatisfactoriness, transience and insubstantiality.

Udana: One of the Buddhist texts.

Uddhacca-kukkucca: One of the Five Hindrances - distraction and remorse, flurry and worry.

Upacara Samadhi: Access (optimum) concentration.

Upatthana: Mindfulness (as a defilement of Vipassana).

Upekkha: Equanimity - one of the four Brahmaviharas.

Uposatha-Sila: The Eight Precepts kept by devout lay people, especially on Buddha days or intensive meditation retreats.

Vedananupassana: Mindfulness of Feelings - one of the Four Foundations of Mindfulness.

Vicikicca: One of the Five Hindrances - doubt and uncertainty.

Vipassana *(Pali)*, **Vipashy-na** *(Skt)*: Insight meditation - seeing the mind and body clearly in the present moment.

Vipassana Kilesas: Defilements of Vipassana meditation.

Viraya *(Pali)*, **Virya** *(Skt)*: Effort, energy.